"How often do we look back on a decision we made, or a situation we handled and think, *'If I knew then what I know now…'* perhaps we would have managed differently, or obtained a better result? Through personal stories, some touching, some sprinkled with humor, Adessa shares wisdom and timeless truths that will inspire you to live freely and securely to walk into the future God has for you!"

-Brittany L. Ketter, *Social Media Specialist PennDel Women*

What people are saying about *Ageless Truths*:

"Adessa writes a sweet book, which is easy to read and filled with good advice, plus Scriptures to back up her thoughts. I love that each generation can cheer on the generation coming up behind them, and this book does just that!"

-Liz DeFrain, *PennDel Ministry Network Women's Director*

"When I first met Adessa at a Women's Conference (way back when), I was so impressed with the wisdom she shared. She made me wish that I had been like her when I was in my thirties. Although our lives were different in many ways, the core of who we are was very similar.

As I read through *Ageless Truths*, I was amazed at the stories that are shared. Not because I could not imagine Adessa going through these situations, but because the situations were so similar to many that I have lived. The beauty of this book is that the lessons are put into writing, are followed through with practical lessons.

Too often we as believers live out a lesson, but soon forget it and do not apply what was learned to the rest of our journey. Not only does Adessa capture the lesson, but makes the application easily remembered and applied. Although I am older than her, I continue to need these reminders and encouragement to stand up for my convictions, to accept my imperfections, and to move forward from my failures."

-Sharon Poole, *PennDel Ministry Network Girls Ministries Director*

"If you're familiar with Adessa's writings, this latest offering will not disappoint! Adessa combines humor, honesty and humility with sound Biblical principles. Each chapter gives plenty to consider and contemplate, and is relevant for women of all ages; I read it along with my school-age, college-age, and adult daughters! Adessa never disappoints!"

-Corinne Thorpe, Mom of 5 girls and 5 boys, Pastor's Wife, member of Women of Purpose Dream Team

"Godly truth and stories from the heart. *Ageless Truths* is an encouragement to women of all ages. This devotional book captures the importance of Holy Spirit's voice in our lives and the unmistakable value of your voice. So many nuggets of truth in each chapter!"

-Bethany Marshall, Author/ Director of Daughters Conference

"If you are looking to read something real, fresh eye opening, and thought provoking, I recommend Adessa's latest book *Ageless Truths*. Adessa's wit, authenticity, charm and love for God's Word really come through on the pages of this book. The stories are engaging and relatable, while also making you take a look inward and shifting your perspective to Gods perspective. I loved it!"

-Kelly Carver, Author and Speaker

Ageless Truths

Lessons I Learned in My Forties that I Wish I Knew in My Twenties

Adessa Holden

Copyright © 2020 Adessa Holden

All rights reserved. No portion of this book may be reproduced, stored in a retrieval system, or transmitted in any form or by any means—electronic, mechanical, photocopy, recording, scanning, or other—except for brief quotations in reviews or articles, without the prior written permission of the author.

Published by 4One Ministries, Inc.

All Scripture quotations, unless otherwise indicated, are taken from the Holy Bible, New International Version®, NIV®. Copyright ©1973, 1978, 1984, 2011 by Biblica, Inc.™ Used by permission of Zondervan. All rights reserved worldwide. www.zondervan.com The "NIV" and "New International Version" are trademarks registered in the United States Patent and Trademark Office by Biblica, Inc.™

Scripture quotations marked (MSG) are taken from THE MESSAGE, copyright © 1993, 1994, 1995, 1996, 2000, 2001, 2002 by Eugene H. Peterson. Used by permission of NavPress. All rights reserved. Represented by Tyndale House Publishers, Inc.

Scripture quotations marked (NLT) are taken from the Holy Bible, New Living Translation, copyright ©1996, 2004, 2007, 2013, 2015 by Tyndale House Founda-tion. Used by permission of Tyndale House Publishers, Inc., Carol Stream, Illinois 60188. All rights reserved.

Scripture verses marked KJV are from the King James Version of the Bible.

Design: James J. Holden

Subject Headings:

1. Healing —Religious aspects—Christianity. 2. Christian life. 3. Christian women—Religious life. I. Title.

ISBN 978-1-7338505-6-8 (paperback)
ISBN 978-1-7338505-7-5 (ebook)

Printed in the United States of America

DEDICATION

To my wonderful brother who read my birthday list and said, *"You should turn this into a book."* Thanks for always encouraging me and thinking I am capable of more than I believe I am capable of doing. You're the best!

CONTENTS

Introduction		11
Chapter 1	If I Like It	13
Chapter 2	It's My life	19
Chapter 3	Ellie	25
Chapter 4	Your Voice Matters	33
Chapter 5	The Power Of Personal Convictions	43
Chapter 6	Trusting Your Instincts	53
Chapter 7	We Need Friends	61
Chapter 8	I Don't Do Drama	71
Chapter 9	Yesterday Does Not Determine Tomorrow	79
Chapter 10	Overcoming Criticism	85
Chapter 11	Who Made You The Boss?	93
Chapter 12	Who Wouldn't Like Me?	101
Chapter 13	Change Of Plans	109

Chapter 14	The Importance Of Flexibility	119
Chapter 15	Hot Flashes Are Real	127
Chapter 16	Be Kind To Yourself	137
Chapter 17	You Can't Do Everything	143
Chapter 18	Life's Not A Competition	151
Chapter 19	You Really Need To Learn To Laugh	159
Chapter 20	You're Never To Old To Be A Daddy's Girl	167
Chapter 21	What Doesn't Kill You	173
Conclusion		179
About The Author		185
Bibliograpy		187

Introduction

It was the evening of my forty-sixth birthday, and I was watching my favorite movie for the umpteenth time. However, I was struggling to concentrate. My mind kept wandering back to the first time I watched the movie and how much has changed.

Actually, I was thinking about how much I've changed.

I've heard so many women over forty say, *"There's just something about turning forty that changes you. It brings so much perspective. So many unnecessary things fall away, and you begin to find peace with yourself."*

This has absolutely been true for me.

The experiences of the past few years have taught me many lessons that I wish I knew earlier in life. Bored with the movie, I started making a list of those ageless lessons. That list eventually turned into this book, which I'm now excited to share with you.

Right from the start, I want to say that this book is not designed for a particular age group: it is for all women.

If you're forty or older, I pray that you'll find inspiration and encouragement to help you make the rest of your life the best of your life.

If you're in your twenties or thirties (or even a teen), I hope you'll take these ageless truths to heart and learn the lessons that I wish I'd learned sooner.

On this journey, I invite you to laugh at my silliness, feel camaraderie in our similar female challenges, and be encouraged to be the woman God created you to be.

Whether you read it on your own or work through it with a group, I pray that you will be inspired by the ageless truth that God loves you, and no matter how young or old you are, He has a plan and purpose for your life.

I'm excited to share my journey with you!

Chapter 1

If I Like It

"If I like it, and Jesus likes it, that's all that matters."

When I was younger, my Dad used this phrase to express his disapproval whenever one of my clothing choices was too loud or colorful for his preference. Since my teenage years fell in the late eighties and early nineties, you can imagine, that happened quite a lot. (Google 'Saved by the Bell' if you are too young to understand what I mean.)

I remember one outfit that I particularly loved. It was a bright yellow blouse with a matching white skirt with black and yellow polka dots all over it. I was so fashionable in the eighties. Whenever I wore it with my bright yellow plastic jewelry (again, an eighties' specialty), I felt like I owned the world. At least until I'd run into my Dad. Then he'd give me a disapproving look and say those magic words: *"If you like it, that's all that matters."*

Of course, I knew that phrase meant: *"You look ridiculous. Why can't you be more demure, quiet, and conservative?"* For years, these words were a source of pain for me. Eventually, they hurt so much, I'd stop him before they even came out. I'd make a joke mocking his response. I tried to pretend that I didn't care, and his words had no effect on me, but inside, they did.

As I grew older, I started changing myself to receive not just my Dad's approval, but also other people's approval. Over time, I began tucking away the girl with the exuberant personality who wanted to be independent and stand out in a crowd, and replace her with someone who blended in. I wanted the approval of other people so badly that I started squashing my personality and turning into a chameleon—being whoever I needed to be to gain the approval of people around me.

Without even realizing it, my motto became, *"If **you** like it, that's all that matters."* Only I wasn't happy, and God wasn't pleased with the fact that I wasn't being who He created me to be. I'm sad to say that this went on for far too many years in my life.

Thankfully, the Holy Spirit allowed some things to happen in my life that helped me find my way back to being myself. It started when He began taking me through a process of inner healing, where I discovered how the choices I made were a direct result of childhood and teenage pain and trauma. As I allowed Him to heal my past, He set me free to be myself in the present. He's helped me learn to love the way God created me and showed me that the only approval I need in life is the approval of my Heavenly Father.

These truths helped me embrace the truth in the words that *"If I like it, (and Jesus likes it), that really is all that matters."*

If I Like It

Before we go any further, let me make it clear that as much as I enjoy the freedom to be myself and express myself, as a woman of God, I choose to submit all of my choices to the caveats of: *"Would this please God and does it line up with His Word?"* Because, above all else, this is the priority in my life.

However, after something passes that test, I've found tremendous freedom in the truth that it doesn't matter what others think or some magazine says I'm supposed to like. Whether it be what I wear or how I decorate my house, all that matters is whether or not I like it.

For instance, I remember the day, just a year or two ago, that I bought my first pair of red pants. Until that point, I'd been wearing mostly black bottoms—navy blue or brown if I was feeling really wild. Since I was no longer the size eight that I was in high school, and I read somewhere that black was slimming and concealing, I went with it.

Then one day, I looked in my closet and thought, *"That's a lot of black."* Even though black may be slimming, it's also sad. I'm not sad.

After far too much deliberation, I took the giant leap and bought my first pair of red pants. (I felt like such a rebel!) Then, even though I knew that black would look slimmer, I bought a pair of white capris. (What a wild child!) But seriously, after years of trying to blend in, dress to gain approval, and look the way *"I'm supposed to look,"* this was a massive step for me.

Looking back at this experience, I can now see that the battle raging inside of me was between the young woman who loved life, loved color, and was filled with exuberance and excitement, and the damaged version of Adessa who had decided to blend in and live for the approval of other people.

Even after years of counseling and overcoming the issues that caused the problem, I learned that it was up to me to begin making choices that would set the real Adessa free to be herself again.

She began to reappear when I took a chance and purchased that pair of red pants. She gained more traction when I bought the blue-flowered sundress. Boy, did she come alive when I decided to take a chance and paint the accent wall in my kitchen purple!

The truth is that my forties have been filled with opportunities to rediscover the woman that God created me to be. Whether it be how I dress, how I decorate my home, the colors I use on my website, or even the stationary I choose to write a letter, I'm learning that as I allow myself to love and embrace the woman God designed me to be, I am honoring God. I am acknowledging that what He created is good— that His choices in creating me had a purpose—and that as I submit to His purposes, He will work out His plan to use my individuality to play a unique role in His kingdom.

As I'm maturing, I'm learning to love the way God created me. More importantly, I'm learning that it really is only God's approval that matters. When I attempt to twist God's design to gain the approval of someone else, it is actually a form of idolatry as I'm putting their opinion above God's. I never want to do this again.

Instead, I am determined to live my life embracing the truth that *"If I like it and JESUS likes it, that really is all that matters."*

Today, I want to encourage you to begin embracing this truth in your own life.

Spend time alone with the Heavenly Father asking Him,

"Are there areas of my life where I have let other people's approval control me and prevent me from being who You created me to be?"

Ask Him to help you be who He designed you to be so that you can fulfill the purpose He has for your life.

Ask yourself: *"How can I begin applying this lesson to my life today?"* Who knows, it might be your day to buy a pair of red pants!!!

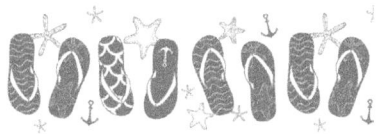

Write in your journal how these verses apply to this chapter's topic:

"Am I now trying to win the approval of human beings, or of God? Or am I trying to please people? If I were still trying to please people, I would not be a servant of Christ." (Galatians 1:10, NIV)

"For you created my inmost being; you knit me together in my mother's womb.

I praise you because I am fearfully and wonderfully made; your works are wonderful, I know that full well.

My frame was not hidden from you when I was made in the secret place, when I was woven together in the depths of the earth.

Your eyes saw my unformed body; all the days ordained for me were written in your book before one of them came to be.

How precious to me are your thoughts, God! How vast is the sum of them! Were I to count them, they would outnumber the grains of sand— when I awake, I am still with you." (Psalm 139:13-18, NIV)

"For we are God's handiwork, created in Christ Jesus to do good works, which God prepared in advance for us to do." (Ephesians 2:10, NIV)

Chapter 2

It's My Life

"One of the best things about being an adult is that you get to choose the life you live."

I was reminded of this truth when a one day *"mental health day"* trip to the beach took an unexpected turn. My brother, Jamie, has a neurological disability that twists his foot. He lives in constant pain and cannot walk on unstable surfaces like sand. However, a few years ago, we found a place at our favorite beach where you could drive on the sand to go fishing. Even though we weren't fishing, we'd drive to this spot to get as close as we could to the ocean without having to walk on the sand.

We didn't realize that while this worked during the off-season (when we usually go), in June the sand is much fluffier, and you need a license to fish. Devoid of these facts, when we tried to drive on to the beach, our tires got stuck in the sand.

As our tires were spinning in the sand and it began to sink in that our car wasn't going to move, I started nervously laughing. Quickly realizing this was not a laughing matter, I panicked and began searching the internet for tips on what to do if you are stuck in the sand. Unfortunately, there were only two options: dig or call a tow. Without a shovel, we were stranded.

So we started praying. God answered our prayer by sending us a park ranger. Now if this were a Hallmark movie, this would have been the "meet cute" where the ranger who happened along turned out to be the man of my dreams. However, this was real life and the ranger who deflated our tires and dug us out, gave us a fine for not having a fishing license. As we were waiting for the citation, holding up other cars because we got stuck in the middle of the road, and praying that the digging would work so we didn't need a tow truck, I thought, *"Well, this is the end of our trip. We drove five hours just to turn around and go home upset because of the fine."*

That was the pattern in my family when I was a little girl. If something happened, it was a catastrophe. My Dad's mood would have changed. He'd have gotten sick, a fight would have ensued, and we'd have driven home in uncomfortable silence. Inside, I could feel myself bracing for this outcome.

Then it occurred to me: I'm the adult. We choose how this story ends. We decide how we respond. That day (after we were out of the sand and we knew the car was fine), we decided that we'd make a different choice. We chose to put our mistake behind us and go on with our trip. No drama. No argument. No tension or assigning blame. We just admitted we were wrong and went back on our way.

As we were driving home later that night, I began thinking about how awesome it is that, as adult women, we can make choices that determine the outcome of our lives. Obviously, this applies to far more important areas than how we respond when we get stuck in the sand at the beach. Instead, we get to choose how we will respond to all situations in life.

We choose how we will spend our time. We choose how we spend our money.

We decide how we want to be treated by what we tolerate in our relationships and with whom we surround ourselves.

If we don't like our job, we can change it.

Don't like the path you're on? You can take a different one. You're never too old to make a change, learn something new, or start a new adventure.

One of the greatest gifts God has given us is free will. Each day, we exercise it as we choose the path for our lives.

The most important decision that I have made in my own life is that I want to live my life completely surrendered to Jesus. This means more than just saying a sinner's prayer and calling myself a Christian. It means that I submit every part of my life to God's will, to commit to living a life worthy of my calling and fulfilling God's purpose for my life.

Part of this commitment means I am committed to understanding and living by the principles taught in the Bible. I believe that the Bible is God's Word. More than just an inspirational book, it is meant to be our guide through life. I take what it says literally. If it says something is sin, then I try to avoid it. When the Bible says to do something, I try my best to make it a part of my life.

Doesn't this make my life a little different than the average American? Doesn't it keep me from doing things others say are acceptable?

Yes.

But I'm okay with that because I believe God's ways are best. Just like I don't want to drink poison, I don't want to do anything that will damage my relationship with God or keep me from walking in His perfect will.

This is my choice. Even though it has required sacrifice throughout the years, I continue to make it over and over again.

Today, as we're near the beginning of our journey, I encourage you to make the same choice. Choose to live your life for Jesus. Submit your life entirely to Him and commit to following the principles in the Bible. Determine that whatever it takes, you will be a radical, sold-out, wholehearted follower of Jesus.

Center your life choices around His will.

It's My Life

Don't just read the Bible: obey it. Develop an intimate, personal relationship with God in prayer.

Commit that, whatever it takes, you will be the woman God created you to be, fulfilling the destiny He has for you in His kingdom. At the end of your life, it's the only decision that matters.

The older I get and the more I walk with Jesus, the more I understand that if God is pleased with me, than life is good. At the end of the day, when you take off your makeup and put on your pj's, you need to be able to look yourself in the mirror and like what you see. You need to be content with yourself, and be able to say with a clear conscience that you did all you could to live a life worthy of your calling.

You need to know that you and God are okay, that you've done all you can to live in a way that pleases Him, that you've avoided sin, and that you are walking in His plan for your life.

It's important that when everything else is stripped away, and you turn off the lights that you can genuinely say it is well with your soul. That is the best choice you will ever make in life.

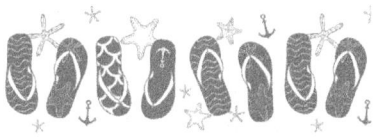

Write in your journal how these verses apply to this chapter's topic.

"So fear the Lord and serve him wholeheartedly. Put away forever the idols your ancestors worshiped when they lived beyond the Euphrates River and in Egypt. Serve the Lord alone.

But if you refuse to serve the Lord, then choose today whom you will serve. Would you prefer the gods your ancestors served beyond the Euphrates? Or will it be the gods of the Amorites in whose land you now live?

But as for me and my family, we will serve the Lord." (Joshua 24:14-15, NLT)

"Therefore I, a prisoner for serving the Lord, beg you to lead a life worthy of your calling, for you have been called by God." (Ephesians 4:1, NLT)

"Dear friends, you always followed my instructions when I was with you. And now that I am away, it is even more important.

Work hard to show the results of your salvation, obeying God with deep reverence and fear.

For God is working in you, giving you the desire and the power to do what pleases him." (Philippians 2:12-13, NLT)

Chapter 3

Ellie

"Don't pretend to be something that you aren't."

A few years ago, I met a woman I will call Ellie. She had it together. Smart, stylish, capable, and confident, Ellie is everything that I wish I could be when I grow up.

Even though Ellie and I are not close at all, we cross each other's path from time to time. Every time it is a complete disaster.

Why? Because I admire Ellie. So much so, that whenever I get around her, I get nervous and tongue-tied. Even though I try to keep my head together, I get so intimidated that I say the stupidest things and usually make no sense. After she walks away, I realize what I said and think, *"What is wrong with you? Why did you say that?"*

Lest you think this is all in my mind, I can assure you I'm not the only one who has noticed this phenomenon. No, my brother has seen it happen so often that he's given it a name. Whenever we see someone on television or in a movie get star struck and act like their mind has taken a vacation when they are around someone they admire, he'll say, *"Look 'Des, they got 'Ellie-d'."* (Aren't brothers awesome?) Every time he sees me talking to Ellie, he just stands back and laughs, wondering what I'll say to embarrass myself this time. And so the story goes.

Most of the time, I try to avoid her because it's just easier. One time I did talk to her without saying anything dumb, and I immediately texted my friend to tell her of my accomplishment. Knowing my silly struggle, my friend was very proud. I was a little proud, too. One intelligent conversation in a decade: not too bad. (Not so great either.)

As I said, the problem isn't with Ellie—it's me. I just admire her so much. If I were God, I would have made me a carbon copy of her—beautiful, collected, able to have a conversation without getting tongue-tied.

However, that wasn't God's plan.

He didn't think the world needed two Ellie's. He felt it needed one of her and one of me.

In my younger days, I thought that the best way I could serve God and live my best life would be to wear a giant Ellie mask and do my best Ellie impersonation. But as I've grown older, I've realized that this is no way to live. Instead, I need to be the unique woman that God made me to be. There may be things I can learn from Ellie or women like her, but my true calling and purpose comes from being myself.

As I talk to other women who have passed the forty-year-old milestone, this is one of the lessons I hear most. So many say, *"The older I get, the more I have learned just to be who I am and not try to pretend I'm someone or something I'm not. It cannot be done."*

How I wish this truth would have settled in my heart earlier in life! Instead, I have to confess that I spent too much of my early life pretending, wearing masks, trying to be the woman I thought people would like and respect. Whenever I saw a woman I admired, I'd try to copy her. I'd dress like her, try to talk like her, and imitate how she did things. Yet, no matter how hard I tried, I could never be just like her. All I could be was a cheap imitation. As we all know, it's easy to spot a reproduction. Real value is only found in authenticity.

Eventually, one of the lessons that I had to learn was that you can not fulfill God's plan or the purpose for your life if you are pretending to be someone or something that you are not. It's just not possible. God created you the way that you are for a purpose. You are the way you are for a reason. No part of your personality, your abilities, your tastes, or even your physical qualities are a mistake. You are uniquely designed for a purpose.

Whenever you pretend to be something that you are not or allow yourself to become a chameleon blending into the circumstances around you, you are telling God that He did something wrong when He created you. You are also lying.

True freedom and true fulfillment come when we stop pretending, stop wearing masks, and start appreciating the way God made us. Until we do this, we are unable to fulfill the amazing plans God has for our lives. However, when we give up fighting God's design and just go with His plan, we find that He created us exactly how we need to be to do what He has called us to do.

How do we do this?

The first thing we need to do is choose to stop wearing masks and decide to be genuine. We have to be honest about ourselves and allow people to know us.

As someone who has a lot of imperfections, I will admit that this can feel risky. I mean, what if I stop pretending and let myself be truly authentic and people don't like me? What if I tell my story, embarrassing parts and all, and they reject me?

Here are some realizations that have helped me answer these thoughts in my life.

First, most people can see through a phony. The odds are, if you're not genuine, if you're always pretending to be something you are not and putting on airs, people aren't buying your act anyway. The fact is that most people have pretty good "imitation detectors." Although we may not know exactly who someone really is, we can tell when someone isn't authentic. Since you're not fooling anyone with

Ellie

your act—you might as well be yourself.

I've observed that most people don't want to be around people who need to act like they always have it all together. Think about it, do you?

Instead, people are drawn to genuine people. Authentic. Real. Most people don't want you to be perfect; however, they do want you to be honest.

In my own life, I've observed that as I've learned to be genuine, be vulnerable, be open about who I am, the good, the bad, and the ugly, people liked me more. As I shared my story, even the parts filled with failure, heartache, and pain, they were able to relate. Others who have similar stories or were experiencing the same feelings began finding hope and encouragement from my openness about my mess.

Rather than people rejecting me, what I found was that the more real I was, the more others could relate. More importantly, the more I allowed myself to simply be who God created, the more He could use me to share His hope and healing with others, and the more people I could reach for Jesus.

It's funny—-I spent so many years trying to make myself into someone else. Yet, it wasn't until I decided to be the most honest version of myself that I was able to fulfill God's plan for my life.

The same is true for all of us.

We can only discover our real purpose in life when we

take off our masks, stop pretending to be someone else, and are bold enough to be ourselves.

It sets us free.

It sets other people free.

It allows the Holy Spirit the freedom to lead us into the unique purpose that God has for our lives.

Write in your journal how these verses apply to this chapter's topic:

"Who in the world do you think you are to second-guess God? Do you for one moment suppose any of us knows enough to call God into question?

Clay doesn't talk back to the fingers that mold it, saying, 'Why did you shape me like this?' Isn't it obvious that a potter has a perfect right to shape one lump of clay into a vase for holding flowers and another into a pot for cooking beans?" (Romans 9:20-21, MSG)

"Thank you for making me so wonderfully complex! Your workmanship is marvelous—how well I know it." (Psalm 139:14, NLT)

Ellie

"Before I formed you in the womb I knew you, before you were born I set you apart; I appointed you as a prophet to the nations." (Jeremiah 1:5, NIV)

"And who knows but that you have come to your royal position for such a time as this?" (Esther 4:14b, NIV)

Chapter 4

Your Voice Matters

"Your voice matters. Don't ever let someone tell you it doesn't."

We met when I was the guest speaker at a Bible study. She was a very confident woman, probably in her late thirties, dressed very well, and so engaging. I could totally relate to the story she told about her trepidation at sharing an unpopular message that the Holy Spirit had placed on her heart. She talked about how she believed the Holy Spirit was challenging her to teach younger women, especially teenage girls, about the need for modesty in their appearance. No, she wasn't extreme at all. Instead, her message was to respect yourself and understand the struggles of brothers in Christ to maintain purity in their thoughts and lives.

As she spoke, it was evident that her motives and passion for the topic were genuine and sincere. Of course, so were the fears that she shared.

She was afraid of seeming too legalistic—she knew everyone had their convictions, and she didn't want to appear judgmental.

She was afraid of being seen as an old-fashioned prude.

She worried that it wasn't the Holy Spirit leading her, but just her own beliefs.

Eventually, she admitted that she was afraid of the response she would get as she shared the incident of a snotty teenage girl telling her, *"You wouldn't feel this way if you looked good in a bikini. You just believe this because you can't pull it off."* (Excuse me while I roll my eyes!)

As she shared, I remembered a similar experience from my thirties. I was teaching a group of ten to thirteen-year-old girls about the importance of only dating Christians and saving physical intimacy for marriage. Honestly, I was surprised that many hadn't heard this teaching before. However, the response wasn't entirely positive. Instead, my seventeen-year-old assistant said, *"Yeah, but if we do that, then we'll end up single like YOU!"*

At the moment, I shook it off and stood my ground, but I have to admit that her words bothered me for weeks afterward. I began thinking, *"Maybe I'm not the best example for these girls. Perhaps they should have a teacher who has everything they want….a husband, a family, a successful career."* Over and over, I questioned whether my voice had value because I was single.

Your Voice Matters

Looking back, I can now see that the real issue wasn't whether my voice had value, but that the enemy, Satan, wanted to quiet my voice so that it wouldn't influence these young girls. Much like my friend, who believes she needs to teach modesty to a generation who may not have ever heard of it before, my voice was speaking God's truth to these young women. There are few things that Satan fears more than God's women speaking God's Word.

Why? Because there is always the possibility that it might take root in someone's heart and change their lives. There's the chance that someone who has never heard what the Bible says will not just listen to it, but also obey it. They will turn from sin, choose God's way, and thwart Satan's plan to destroy their lives.

There's also the possibility that someone who knows the right thing to do but is wavering in their commitment to do it, will be encouraged to stand firm. Over the years, I've observed that many believers who have had proper training in the Word of God are worried that they are too legalistic, too judgmental, and too old-fashioned. They are afraid that they are the only ones who believe such things, so they either keep quiet or start to compromise their convictions to be part of the church crowd. Yet, as soon as they hear another voice reinforcing their beliefs, they are encouraged to stand firm. Remembering that they are not alone, they regain the courage to continue doing what they know is right. Some even gain the courage to add their voice now that they know they are not alone.

However, these are not the stories that the enemy wants

you to hear.

Instead, whenever we feel the Holy Spirit leading us to share God's Word, to speak out for injustice, to differentiate between right and wrong, or even to share our testimony with someone, he immediately tries to fill us with fear. Suddenly, our minds are filled with *"what-if's."*

"What if they laugh at you?"

"What if they don't invite you to the next Ladies' Event?"

"What if they think you are too legalistic? Remember, the Bible says we live under 'grace'". (Seriously, this is one of the biggest lies the enemy uses to silence truth among God's people. Because while we are saved by grace, as followers of Christ, the Bible still commands us to live by the truth in God's Word. Grace gives us freedom from sin, not freedom to sin.)

"What if they reject you?"

I find this particularly true when it comes to speaking truth to close friends and family members. Sadly, this *"what-if"* has kept too many Christian parents from speaking necessary truth into the lives of their children. The fear of rejection is powerful. Yet, if we truly love someone, we need to speak truth into their lives.

Other *"what-if's"* are:

"What if I'm wrong?"

"What if they turn on me and use my testimony against me,

and I'm embarrassed?"

"What if my voice doesn't matter or make a difference?"

Here are some things that I have learned on my journey through struggling with these "what-if's":

1. If you truly believe God has told you to share something, you must be obedient.

Sometimes I think we underestimate the value of obedience in the modern Church. It is far more important than we acknowledge. If you truly believe the Holy Spirit is calling you to speak into a situation, then your only choices are to obey or disobey God. The "what-if's" don't matter. As a follower of Christ, you are under an obligation to do what God has told you to do and let the results to Him.

2. Remember the parable of the soils.

In Matthew 13, Jesus tells the story of a farmer who went out to sow his seed in different soils. Some of the seed fell on land that was so hard that it produced no crop. Other seed started to take root, but the weeds took over and destroyed it. Finally, there was the seed that fell on the good ground. This seed produced an enormous crop that gave the farmer income.

This parable explains the process of what happens whenever we use our voice to share God's truth or the testimony of what God has done in our lives. True, some may reject it. Others may hear what we're saying, but eventually, blow it off and do what they want.

As we see in the parable of the soils, there is always the possibility that some seeds will take root. There's the strong possibility that God is leading you to speak to that one heart that needs to hear, that wants to respond, and that will be strongly impacted by what you have to say. We continue using our voice even when we are rejected by some, in the belief that God will use our words to reach the one—the good soil who will produce a harvest.

3. Your testimony doesn't belong to you.

One of the most powerful ways that we can use our voice is to share our testimony of what God has done in our lives. Ironically, this is also one of the scariest things to do because it means that we have to be vulnerable with our story and share personal information without knowing how people will respond. If you're like me and you grew up in a house that said, *"What happens inside the home stays inside the home,"* it can be a real struggle to share part of yourself that isn't exactly flattering or shares family secrets.

Early in our ministry, this was a big struggle for me. Fear of what people would think or betraying family members by sharing my story kept me from using my voice the way God desired. I'll never forget the night I attended a conference, and the Holy Spirit used a speaker who was extremely vulnerable with their story to teach me that my testimony did not belong to me. Instead, it belonged to God. It was the story of His redemption, His grace, His healing, and His ability to change lives. Because of all He has done for us, out of an attitude of gratefulness, each of us has the responsibility to share our testimony with others so they can find hope that

God can do the same thing for them.

Revelations 12:11 says, *"They triumphed over him by the blood of the Lamb and by the word of their testimony."*

The truth is that your testimony has the power to change lives. Don't let the lies of the enemy keep you from using your voice to share God's story with other people. Remember, the enemy doesn't want people's lives changed for the better, and he doesn't want people to spend eternity in Heaven.

4. Your voice is powerful.

This brings us to our final truth: your voice is powerful. That is why Satan tries so hard to keep you from using it. That's why he throws fear, worry, doubt, and insecurity at you like fiery darts—-in the hopes that you will keep quiet.

However, this is not God's will for His daughters. Instead, He wants us to use our voices to speak the truth, whether it is popular or not. God's will is for you to share your story so that others can find hope and a relationship with Jesus through your testimony.

God's will is for His daughters to stand up for righteousness, speak out against injustice, be a voice for those who cannot speak for themselves, share the truth, share hope, and be a light in a very dark world.

God gave you a voice for a reason.

Though doubt, fear, and insecurity may try to quiet you, though some may even say your voice doesn't matter or is insignificant, these are all lies from an enemy that knows just how powerful your voice can be.

Your voice matters.

Don't ever let someone tell you it doesn't. God gave you a voice. He gave you insight. He's given you a perspective. He wants to use your story as a testimony to bring people to Him. Don't let fear, intimidation, or embarrassment steal your voice. Never let anyone tell you that your voice doesn't matter or isn't worth being heard. Don't let anyone steal it or silence your voice.

Instead, use it for God's glory, to advance His kingdom, to encourage other people, and to fulfill the purpose He has for your life.

Write in your journal how these verses apply to this chapter's topic:

"They triumphed over him by the blood of the Lamb and by the word of their testimony." (Revelations 12:11, NIV)

"Then he told them many things in parables, saying: 'A farmer went out to sow his seed.

As he was scattering the seed, some fell along the path, and the birds came and ate it up.

Some fell on rocky places, where it did not have much soil. It sprang up quickly, because the soil was shallow.

But when the sun came up, the plants were scorched, and they withered because they had no root.

Other seed fell among thorns, which grew up and choked the plants.

Still other seed fell on good soil, where it produced a crop— hundred, sixty or thirty times what was sown.

Whoever has ears, let them hear…..Listen then to what the parable of the sower means: When anyone hears the message about the kingdom and does not understand it, the evil one comes and snatches away what was sown in their heart. This is the seed sown along the path.

The seed falling on rocky ground refers to someone who hears the word and at once receives it with joy.

But since they have no root, they last only a short time. When trouble or persecution comes because of the word, they quickly fall away.

The seed falling among the thorns refers to someone who hears the word, but the worries of this life and the deceitfulness of wealth choke the word, making it unfruitful.

But the seed falling on good soil refers to someone who hears the word and understands it. This is the one who produces a crop, yielding a hundred, sixty or thirty times what was sown.'" (Matthew 13:3-9 and 18-23, NIV)

"Then the Lord reached out his hand and touched my mouth and said to me, 'I have put my words in your mouth. See, today I appoint you over nations and kingdoms to uproot and tear down, to destroy and overthrow, to build and to plant.'" (Jeremiah 1:9-10, NIV)

"Speak up for those who cannot speak for themselves, for the rights of all who are destitute. Speak up and judge fairly; defend the rights of the poor and needy." (Proverbs 31:8-9, NIV)

"She speaks with wisdom, and faithful instruction is on her tongue." (Proverbs 31:26, NIV)

Chapter 5

The Power of Personal Convictions

"Getting older has taught me how necessary it is to have personal convictions."

Even though I'm not a huge fan of the Captain America movies, when I heard the following quote from *Captain America: Civil War*, it stood out to me.

"Compromise where you can. Where you can't, don't. Even if everyone is telling you that something wrong is something right. Even if the whole world is telling you to move, it is your duty to plant yourself like a tree, look them in the eye, and say 'No, you move'." — Christopher Markus[1]

The older I get, the more I believe in the importance of

having strong personal convictions—unshakeable beliefs that you are willing to fight for, to die for, or more commonly to stand firm on.

I say that standing firm happens more often because, at least until now, most Christians in America have not had to take civil action, go to prison, or risk death for their faith as so many who have gone before us. I'm well aware that this may change in the days ahead; however, it isn't a common experience for now.

Instead, most believers today are called to *"stand firm"*—to plant themselves like a tree against family, friends, and a society that calls us to be *"tolerant."* Essentially, they want us to *"bend."* They implore us to be *"flexible"* on essential convictions that are immovable.

Among these convictions are the beliefs that:

- There is only One God, and He created the universe.

- All religions are not equal. The only way to achieve salvation and spend eternity in Heaven is by accepting Jesus as your personal Savior and repenting of your sin.

- Even though grace is free, Christians are called to live in a way that pleases God.

- The Bible is the infallible Word of God.

- The Bible is still relevant and applicable today. We still need to obey what it says.

- If the Bible calls something "sin," it is "sin," no matter what

The Power Of Personal Convictions

society says. This includes so many of the prevalent sins that our world now glorifies as normal, socially acceptable, and modern.

As Christians living in the twenty-first century, these convictions are frequently coming under attack. Still, they are areas where we cannot compromise but must, as the quote says, *"Plant ourselves like a tree and say, 'I'm not moving.'"*

Of course, when it comes to the topic of convictions, these are the obvious points. The less obvious and often more difficult situations to face are the real-life circumstances where it would be genuinely easier to compromise our personal beliefs than take a stand. It's the areas where our thoughts tell us, *"It's no big deal—it isn't life or death—just a little compromise will make your life so much easier"* that tend to trip us up.

It's the temptation to stop obeying the Bible and tithing 10% of your income when you're going through financial difficulty.

It agrees to pay someone under the table even though you know it's illegal.

It's choosing to lie just to keep things simpler.

It's compromising your conviction to go along with the crowd or avoid offending someone.

These are the times that cause the rubber to meet the road as we ask ourselves, *"Am I a woman who is guided by her convictions, or do I flounder and abandon my convictions when the going gets tough?"*

Throughout my life, I have always believed that I was a woman of strong convictions. I've always been passionate about what I believed and done my best to stand by those convictions, no matter what. And yet, it wasn't until I reached my late thirties or early forties that I truly saw the importance of identifying my convictions. By that, I mean taking time to sit down and make a list of beliefs and convictions that I was unwilling to bend on. As always, this decision was the result of hard times—moments when people asked me to *"bend,"* and I realized I just could not.

In my late thirties and early forties, these options presented themselves over and over again. One of the first times was when we received an invitation to attend a same-sex wedding. It was a few months after my Mom died, and trust me when I say that my Mom would not have received that invite! She was a woman of strong convictions, and everyone knew she wouldn't go.

However, Mom was in Heaven, and people were wondering whether Jamie and I would hold to her convictions or take a more liberal approach. They didn't have to wonder for long. I could not compromise what I believed and attend the ceremony even though I loved the people getting married and prayed for them.

The next big challenge came when our very old car began giving us trouble. The standard advice was, *"Trade it in for a newer one."* The only problem was that we had committed to following Dave Ramsey's Total Money Makeover principles

The Power Of Personal Convictions

and avoiding debt. Not only had we made this commitment, but I was teaching on the topic. Only now it wasn't theoretical—I had to decide to practice what I preached or compromise. We chose to get the car fixed and keep saving money. Years later, God honored our decision and helped us find a fantastic car at an unbelievably low price. Still, that was **after** we chose to stand firm to our convictions.

These challenges were nothing compared to what we would face in the future as Christians, fellow believers, were the ones asking us to compromise. Using arguments like *"It's no big deal if you just don't report that money to the IRS"* or *"Why do you have to be so legalistic in your choices of entertainment?"*, time and again I have been forced to be brave, put on my big girl pants, and say, *"I'm sorry, I can't compromise."*

The hardest one for me was when a friend that I deeply admire and trusted told me to change a message that I truly believed the Holy Spirit asked me to share. For weeks, we went back and forth as she tried to convince me I was wrong, and she was right. This was truly heart-wrenching for me because I loved my friend and hated having to say *"no"* to her. I spent so much time praying about this situation, but I felt no release to make a change.

Eventually, my friend apologized and admitted that she was wrong, but until we got there, the struggle inside of me was real! I didn't like standing up to my friend, and yet, she was asking me to go against a personal conviction. I just couldn't do it.

Why? Because deep inside, I knew that if I *"bent"* and compromised my deep conviction, I would be disobeying God and compromising my integrity.

At the end of the day, I'm the one who has to look in the mirror and respect what I see. I'm the one who is going before God in prayer, knowing that I put pleasing someone else over pleasing Him. Ultimately, I'm the one who will have to give account to God for my life. This includes every decision, every word, and every compromise. (Matthew 12:36-37) When that day comes, I want to hear Him say, *"Well done,"* not *"What were you thinking?"*.

This is why I believe it is so vital for all of us to be women of conviction. Each of us needs to identify what we believe and how far we are willing to go to stand by those beliefs.

One thing that helped me through this process was sitting down and making a list of beliefs that I could not compromise. Obviously, this list included the essential beliefs I listed at the top; however, it also contained personal convictions that I cannot abandon.

It's so important that we don't minimize the value of personal convictions, even if they seem insignificant in the grand scheme of things. Because over the years, I have learned that how we respond when our personal convictions are questioned, helps us prepare for the times when our concrete beliefs are attacked.

There's a Scripture in Jeremiah that says,

> **"If you have raced with men on foot and they**

The Power Of Personal Convictions

have worn you out, how can you compete with horses? If you stumble in safe country, how will you manage in the thickets by the Jordan?"
(Jeremiah 12:5, NIV)

In this passage, Jeremiah was complaining to God about all he suffered because He was God's prophet. Rather than saying, *"Oh, poor Jeremiah,"* God spoke these words, which essentially say, *"You ain't seen nothing yet. If you aren't strong enough to stand up to a little suffering, what are you going to do when major persecution comes?"* (My paraphrase, but if you read a commentary, that's the gist.)

Here's how the principle applies to us: I believe that sometimes God allows us to experience a little suffering as we stand up for our personal convictions to teach us how to stand firm in the face of significant persecution regarding the unshakeable truths of God's kingdom. Every time we stand firm in our convictions, we grow stronger. Our convictions deepen. We are less likely to *"bend"* with every new theory and more likely to stand firm and say, *"No, you move."*

I've seen this happen in my own life. Even though I've always wanted to be a woman with deep convictions, it wasn't until my beliefs were tested that I could really claim the title. As is true with so much, it is the difficulties in life that make us shine—be who we genuinely are—and fulfill our purpose in life.

That's why, as I look back on my life, I'm thankful for the challenges to my convictions. They made me stronger. They proved to me that God honors our faithfulness to Him and

Ageless Truths

His Word. They helped me understand what it means to plant yourself like a tree and stand firm.

Write in your journal how these verses apply to this chapter's topic:

"Consider it pure joy, my brothers and sisters, whenever you face trials of many kinds, because you know that the testing of your faith produces perseverance.

Let perseverance finish its work so that you may be mature and complete, not lacking anything.

If any of you lacks wisdom, you should ask God, who gives generously to all without finding fault, and it will be given to you.

But when you ask, you must believe and not doubt, because the one who doubts is like a wave of the sea, blown and tossed by the wind. That person should not expect to receive anything from the Lord. Such a person is double-minded and unstable in all they do." (James 1:2-8, NIV)

"Therefore, my dear brothers and sisters, stand firm. Let nothing move you. Always give yourselves fully to the work of the Lord, because you know that your labor in the Lord is not in vain." (1 Corinthians 15:58, NIV)

The Power Of Personal Convictions

"Be on your guard; stand firm in the faith; be courageous; be strong." (1 Corinthians 16:13, NIV)

"But I tell you that everyone will have to give account on the day of judgment for every empty word they have spoken. For by your words you will be acquitted, and by your words you will be condemned." (Matthew 12:36-37, NIV)

"So then, each of us will give an account of ourselves to God." (Romans 14:12, NIV)

Chapter 6

Trusting Your Instincts

"The older I get, the more I learn to trust my instincts instead of doubting them. More times than not, they are right."

Have you ever been in a situation where that little voice inside of you seems to be screaming, "*Danger!! Danger!! Stay away! This is wrong*"?

I think we've all been there. Since my late thirties, I have been there several times.

One of the first times that comes to my mind involved a job. At first glance, it looked like a fantastic opportunity. Yet, in the days that followed, everything inside of me started feeling like something was wrong. For days, I just couldn't shake this *"Do Not Enter"* feeling.

The only problem was that I was too young and insecure at the time to trust my instincts. Instead, I blamed myself for negative feelings.

I told myself I was just scared.

I chastised myself for being too self-absorbed, too competitive, too jealous to want to be part of the team.

I even thought maybe it was just hormones making me feel so upset.

It turns out it was none of those things. How I wish now I would have recognized the Holy Spirit's voice speaking to me and walked away from the whole situation. Instead, I ignored my instincts, and the job was a nightmare. Thankfully, I learned a lot of lessons, chief of which was: learn to listen to the little voice inside.

The next experience that comes to my mind involved not a job, but a person. Even though this person had exemplary credentials and was loved and respected by other people, every time I was around him, an alarm went off inside of me. Honestly, I felt absolutely ridiculous! Everyone else thought he was the greatest guy in the world. Even people we trusted said I had to get over it, I was wrong, he was completely trustworthy. Yet, over and over again, that part of me that recognizes an abusive man kept sounding the alarm.

Again, I doubted myself.

I thought, *"You're just superimposing your issues from your past with your Dad onto him."*

Trusting Your Instincts

I told myself I had issues with men (even though this was the only man who made me feel afraid).

I questioned myself, doubted myself, and wondered what my problem was over and over again.

Only this time, I didn't make the same mistake I made with the job. Instead of ignoring my instincts, I decided to keep my distance. I wasn't *"all-in"* or *"all-out."* I made sure all of my interactions with him involved my brother because this feeling just wouldn't go away.

Well, as time would tell, eventually, this man did show his true colors. I decided that going forward; I would never doubt my instincts again.

Instead, what I've learned from these situations and others like them is that the Holy Spirit uses our instincts to warn us of danger. Often, that little voice inside of us is the Holy Spirit speaking to us, trying to protect us from a difficult situation. It's His voice saying, *"This is a problem—stay away—-do not enter."*

As it says in John 16:13, one of the Holy Spirit's functions is to guide us in truth.

> *"When the Spirit of truth comes, he will guide you into all truth. He will not speak on his own but will tell you what he has heard. He will tell you about the future." (NLT)*

As born again, Spirit-filled women, we need to learn to listen to the voice of the Holy Spirit as He tries to lead us, rather than ignore His warnings. I understand that it's hard. We wonder, *"Is this the Holy Spirit talking to me? How can I be sure? What if it isn't Him and I make a wrong decision? What if it is just a prejudice or predisposition on my part?"*

Here are a few things I've learned regarding these questions.

First, to the issue of instincts. What if it isn't the Holy Spirit, but our own experiences causing a natural reaction to certain stimuli?

I think the first question we have to ask ourselves is, *"Why is that a bad thing?"*

Didn't God give us instincts when He created us?

Doesn't God know the things you've gone through in your life?

Isn't He able to redeem the things that were once a source of pain and heartache in your life, heal you, and now make those same things a source of wisdom?

Isn't it possible that as a born-again woman led by the Holy Spirit, God could be using your instincts to guide you in certain situations? If God could use a donkey to stop Balaam, couldn't He use the instincts He's given you to warn you of danger? (Numbers 22)

The problem is too often we mistrust ourselves. When we feel like a circumstance may be problematic, we often question our motivation to feel that way, especially if we are the only ones who are uncomfortable in a situation.

Trusting Your Instincts

Yet, what I have learned is that as a woman who seeks to live her life under the control of the Holy Spirit, my first response needs to change from *"What is wrong with me that I feel this way?"* to *"Why is God allowing me to feel this way?"*.

This leads right into the second lesson, and that is the importance of learning to proceed with caution.

Again, time and maturity have taught me that as I ask God to help me sort out my feelings, the best thing to do is to slow down.

I've learned that there is never a need to make a quick decision. If I feel uncomfortable with something or that inner alarm is going off, I've learned to see it as a warning light on my car. It's time to slow down, to check things out, and investigate before I proceed.

For instance, if we're about to make a purchase and everything inside of my is screaming, then we wait until another day. Time will tell whether it was the Holy Spirit trying to say, *"Don't buy this,"* or whether it was just a passing fear on my part. Sometimes, it's just the Holy Spirit saying, *"Wait"* because a better deal or a better option is coming in the next few weeks.

Maybe you're asked out on a date, and your alarm says, *"I don't trust this guy."* Saying *"maybe another time"* gives you time to get to know him better. If it's God's will, he'll ask again and your heart will change. If it's a Holy Spirit warning, you'll be glad you declined.

Perhaps your daughter is invited to a sleepover, and you're

the only Mom who doesn't feel comfortable with the situation. Trust me; there will be another sleepover. Your caution alarm may save her a world of heartache.

These are just a few examples from a plethora of circumstances that illustrate that there's no need to be in a hurry. Looking back on the first story about the nightmare job, I now see that if I'd have just slowed down and taken time to be cautious, I could have avoided the whole situation.

What do you do while you're cautious?

Pray. Earnestly pray about the situation. God can change your heart if it is a fear or doubt issue on your part. This happened several times with me when my first instinct was fear. As I've slowed down and prayed about a situation, He's shown me my anxiety and given me the courage to follow Him in faith.

On the other hand, the Holy Spirit can also confirm His warning to you if He is trying to keep you from a bad experience. I am a firm believer that God wants to reveal His truth to His children. He will go out of His way to guide you in the direction He wants you to go. As you slow down and seek His will, He will speak to your heart through Scripture, in prayer, and through the words of others. Because He wants to guide your life, He is more than willing to confirm His will. That's why we must keep our eyes and our ears open.

Looking back on my situations, I can see that in addition to that *"Danger!"* feeling I was experiencing, the Holy Spirit was also providing confirmations to support that instinct. In some circumstances, friends came to me and shared

Trusting Your Instincts

information that served as a warning. In another situation, no matter how often I tried to ignore my feelings and strengthen my friendship with a person, it just didn't happen. It was like a door slammed in my face over and over again. Now I can see that it was the Holy Spirit protecting me.

I have learned for sure that whenever I have pushed aside my doubt and listened to that little voice inside of my that screamed, *"Danger! Stay Away"*, I have never regretted it. The older I get, the more I am learning to trust my instincts more and more. Whether it be the Holy Spirit leading me or the Holy Spirit using my instincts to guide me, I'm learning to trust my gut.

One of the best lessons we can learn is to stop and use caution.

Trust that God is using your instincts to protect you and work all things together for your good.

Stop, look, listen, and trust your instincts.

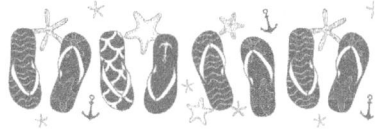

Write in your journal how these verses apply to this chapter's topic:

"When the Spirit of truth comes, he will guide you into all truth. He will not speak on his own but will tell you what he has heard. He will tell you about the future." (John 16:13, NLT)

"I will instruct you and teach you in the way you should go; I will counsel you with my loving eye on you." (Psalm 32:8)

"My sheep listen to my voice; I know them, and they follow me." (John 10:27, NLT)

"Your own ears will hear him. Right behind you a voice will say, 'This is the way you should go,' whether to the right or to the left." (Isaiah 30:21, NLT)

"Your word is a lamp to guide my feet and a light for my path." (Psalm 119:105, NLT)

Chapter 7

We Need Friends

"We all need just a few people in our lives that we trust implicitly—our inner circle."

You don't have to be on the planet very long before you learn that you can't trust everyone. Most females learn at a pretty early age that you have to be very careful about who you tell what, especially when it comes to secrets.

I learned this lesson when I was fifteen and told a girl who said she was my friend which boy I had a crush on at school. Yep, you guessed it. By Monday morning, everyone in our small Christian school knew how I felt. He and I were both embarrassed. It was your typical high school scene right out of *Mean Girls*. The only one who was happy was the nasty girl in the corner, delighting in my misfortune.

I grew up a lot that day. Some times, I'm surprised it took me that long to learn the meaning of *"frenemy."* Over time, I learned even more things like:

Beware of gossips: they don't care about you; they just want the information to share.

Watch out for jealous girls—they are always marking and protecting their territory.

Some girls will stab you in the back just to advance their agenda.

Others will use what you tell them as weapons against you to hurt you.

If a woman talks to you about someone else, be careful. The odds are that she'll be talking to someone else about you soon.

Drama queens who continuously play the victim probably play a more significant part in the problem than they admit or tell you.

Cliques are nasty and mean girls are real, even in the church.

These are just some of the lessons we all eventually learn as we interact with other women and realize you can't trust everyone. The problem is that sometimes this truth makes us feel so hurt and vulnerable that we build a wall around ourselves and decide not to trust anyone. This isn't healthy.

God did not mean for us to go through life alone. That's

why He created the church to operate as a body—walking through life together.

"But 'Des, I've tried that, and I've been hurt over and over again. I don't want to try anymore."

Trust me when I say that I understand. Oh, the stories I could tell of relationships gone wrong and heartaches I've endured because Christian women chose to act in a way that was very un-Christlike. (That's a super-spiritual way of saying they were downright nasty!)

I've been tempted to say, "*I'm done—I'll never trust again.*"

To a point, I haven't. As I've matured, I've learned the importance of protecting myself from dangerous women. I've learned to be cautious about what I share, particularly when I'm going through a hard time. If I share about a difficult time, it's because I'm over it, and it doesn't bother me anymore. It was a different story while I was going through it—then I kept it to myself.

I'm not the girl who will pour out her heart at a Women's Meeting. (I don't know all the people there, why would I trust them?) I stopped going to a meeting after they put me in a small group of strangers and asked us deeply personal questions. I couldn't wait to get out of there! You'll rarely find me giving prayer requests on a prayer chain.

Why? I've learned over the years to guard my heart.

However, this doesn't mean that I don't share. I'm just

extremely selective about when and with whom I share. Even though time has taught me to guard my heart, it has also taught me the absolute necessity of close friends. I firmly believe that we all need just a few people in our lives that we trust implicitly—our inner circle.

They are our kindred spirits—the people who love us and will keep our confidences, protect us no matter what, and always have our backs.

These are the friends who will tell you the truth in love to your face because they want the best for you. They don't talk behind your back, but will tell you straight out where you can improve. These friends will listen to your fears, laugh at your mistakes, and open their hearts to you.

Granted, friends like this are few and far between, but aren't all treasures? Perhaps their rarity is what makes them most valuable.

I am very blessed to have a few of these people in my life. Including my brother, who is my best friend, I would count five. Although I know these people aren't perfect (that happens when you let your hair down with people—you both see each other's flaws), they are trustworthy, reliable, and truly good friends. I know that they are a gift from God because real friends are hard to find. Yet, they are so necessary.

Especially as women, we need friends. We need our girl time. We need people who will listen to us process our emotions, talk through ideas, and hear our hearts.

We need girlfriends we can laugh with and share our silly

We Need Friends

stories. We need honest opinions about whether or not a dress looks bad or we should cut our hair. We need a voice of reason when the hormones are raging—or at least an encouraging voice that says, *"I have hot flashes, too."*

There are times when we need another woman to listen like only a female can and relate to what we are saying. Sometimes we need another woman to hold us accountable, challenge us, and say, *"Girl, what are you thinking?"*

When God created women, He designed us as relational creatures. We need people. Just because we've experienced bad female friendships doesn't mean we should abandon the concept. We simply have to make wiser choices.

No, we can't trust everyone, but we can trust some.

As the Holy Spirit brings godly, trustworthy women into our lives, we need to leave the door open to form relationships. Sure, it's okay to build slowly and tread lightly. That's probably wise, and people will show you who they are with time. But this principle goes both ways. Mean girls will show themselves mean, but real friends will prove they are trustworthy.

Ecclesiastes 4:9-10 says: **"Two are better than one, because they have a good return for their labor: If either of them falls down, one can help the others up." (NIV)**

The older I get, the more I understand this verse and the truth that we all need a few good friends as we walk through life.

Perhaps, like me, you've gone through difficult times and been burned by female friendships. Maybe you've been tempted to give up and say, *"Who needs it?"*

The answer is: you do. All of us need our girls.

Can I encourage you to try again?

Start by asking God to bring a sincere, trustworthy, godly friend into your life. When He answers, be open to the possibility.

Yes, it's okay to go slow and get to know if someone is trustworthy. It's also essential that you are a reliable friend.

Don't be surprised if the friends that God brings you don't come in the demographics you expected. They may be older, younger, married, or single. Their life experiences may be different from your own, and yet, God knows they are what you need. The truth is that all of my closest friends are very different from me. However, in our hearts, we are kindred spirits. I am thankful for each of them.

One of my favorite quotes from Anne of Green Gables says, *"Kindred spirits are not so scarce as I used to think. It's splendid to find out there are so many of them in the world."* [1]

The problem is that along the way to finding kindred spirits, many of us run into mean girls. My encouragement to you today: don't let the mean girls you've met stop you from embracing kindred spirits. I know it's a temptation, but I'm also thankful that I didn't let bad experiences keep me from one of God's greatest gifts—godly friends.

We Need Friends

If you have real, blue, honest to goodness friends, treasure them. Be kind to them. Thank God for them because they make life so much better. Especially as we get older, we need friends.

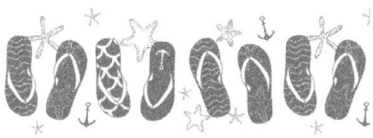

Write in your journal how these verses apply to this chapter's topic:

"As iron sharpens iron, so one person sharpens another." (Proverbs 27:17, NIV)

"The righteous choose their friends carefully, but the way of the wicked leads them astray." (Proverbs 12:26, NIV)

"Better is open rebuke than hidden love. Wounds from a friend can be trusted, but an enemy multiplies kisses." (Proverbs 27:5-6, NIV)

"Perfume and incense bring joy to the heart, and the pleasantness of a friend springs from their heartfelt advice." (Proverbs 27:9, NIV)

"How good and pleasant it is when God's people live together in unity!" *(Psalms 133:1, NIV)*

"Two are better than one, because they have a good return for their labor: If either of them falls down, one can help the other up. But pity anyone who falls and has no one to help them up.

Also, if two lie down together, they will keep warm. But how can one keep warm alone? Though one may be overpowered, two can defend themselves. A cord of three strands is not quickly broken." *(Ecclesiastes 4:9-12, NIV)*

Chapter 8

I Don't Do Drama

"I'll help anyone through a genuine heartache or trauma, but I'm not riding the roller coaster of anyone else's unnecessary drama anymore. It's too exhausting, and they don't want a solution anyway—-they just want to be dramatic. Now that I'm in my forties, I'm not attending the performance."

The older I get, the more I am sure of one thing: I don't have time for unnecessary drama.

I don't like it. It doesn't benefit me, and whenever possible, I don't want it to be a part of my life.

I know, some women love it—-they thrive on it. They play their role as a drama queen in every relationship and situation in their lives. That is their choice. However, the more I live, the more I am sure that this is not who I want to be.

Instead, I want to walk in peace, and I want to bring peace to the people and circumstances around me. I've lived through enough genuine trauma and heartache in my life, that I don't need to create more of it. As I've entered into middle age (that's hard to type), I've decided that drama is one of the childish things that I want to leave behind me.

As Paul said in 1 Corinthians 13:11, ***"When I was a child, I talked like a child, I thought like a child, I reasoned like a child. When I became a man, I put the ways of childhood behind me."***

Before we go further, please allow me to clarify that I am talking about unnecessary drama. I completely understand that life is filled with heartache and genuine trauma that we can often not avoid. I'll help anyone through a genuine heartache or trauma. I will be there for them to listen, to cry, to pray, and to help in any way that I am able. That's not what this chapter is about.

Instead, this chapter is about deciding that when your local drama queen puts on a performance, you will not be attending. Even more, it's about how we can avoid being a drama queen, and instead, be a woman who walks in peace.

This was a decision I made in my late thirties and early forties after a few experiences with drama queens who seemed to create chaos in every situation they entered. After experiencing the tornado of their drama over and over again, I decided I didn't want this to be a part of my life. I began creating boundaries that helped me stop their drama from influencing my life and stealing my peace. Today, I'll share them with you:

1. **Get the Facts**

Something I've learned about drama queens is that they choose to act from a place of emotion rather than facts. Something happens, and they become overwhelmed, panicked, and hysterical before they are even aware of the facts in a situation.

I experience this all the time with my Dad (who, though a male, tends to be very dramatic). For instance, a few months ago, our furnace was leaking. When the repairman came, my Dad came up from the basement wearing his dramatic face and said, *"This is gonna cost big money…it's gonna break the bank."*

At that moment, I had a choice. I could panic and join his dramatic party, or I could wait until the repairman was finished and deal with the facts of the situation. An hour later, the repairman gave me a bill for $150. While $150 isn't nothing, in the world of furnace repair, it was actually a blessing. No tragedy. No drama. No need to be panicked.

Living with my Dad, I've learned that this is a pattern in his life. If I want to avoid being pulled into his drama and constantly riding an emotional roller coaster, I need to choose to meet each problem with calm, wait until the facts are gathered, and then determine how to solve the issue.

2. Avoid Procrastination

Nothing creates drama like waiting until the last minute to complete a task. An easy project becomes an emergency as you race against the clock in an attempt to meet a deadline. Suddenly, your adrenaline is pumping, your heart is racing, and your blood pressure is rising. While some people love the exhilaration, I don't. I've learned to lower the level of drama by simply planning and avoiding procrastination.

Over time, I also learned to set boundaries with dramatic people. For instance, over the last decade, I've had many people write for my website. A few of them struggled with procrastination, which ultimately affected my life. I remember one woman who would always send her submissions just before midnight the day before they were to be posted. This meant that I had to stay up late waiting to see if she'd meet her deadline or I needed to post something else. If she submitted something, I had to work in the wee hours of the morning as she slept.

Then I heard a minister share the line, *"Your procrastination is not my emergency"* and realized that I didn't have to allow her procrastination to cause such drama in my life. Instead, I set boundaries and said, *"If you don't submit your work during working hours, I'm not using it, and I'm not paying for it."*

Drama ended. And it was amazing how much earlier she could submit her work when getting paid was tied to a deadline.

I Don't Do Drama

3. Manipulation

Nothing creates more drama and chaos than a person who chooses to use manipulation to try to control a situation. As Hallmark movies should have already taught us, playing games, going behind people's backs, lying, and scheming only results in drama, pain, and heartache.

Again, these are the tools of the immature. As mature, godly women, we need to choose the path of honesty. We need to be women who choose to work in the light, not in the shadows. As women of God, we should never, ever use our womanly wiles to get what we want or control a situation. Instead, we should be honest, direct, and above board in all of our dealings.

Not only will this path help us be positive representatives of Jesus and gain the respect of others, but it will also keep us from having to clean up the inevitable mess that will come when our deceit or manipulation unravel. (Don't kid yourself—it always unravels.)

4. Gossip and Getting Involved in Other People's Conflicts

We've all been there. Nancy and Susie had a fight, and Nancy can't wait to tell you all about it. *"Susie is horrible. Can you believe she did this? How could she? Well, I know how she could. I've heard she'd done it before…"* On and on, the gossip spreads.

The older I get, the more I have resolved that I don't want to be a part of this type of drama. If Nancy comes to me with a problem with Susie, I'm going to pray with her and tell her the Biblical truth that, *"You need to go talk to Susie."*

I'm not going to choose sides, get in the middle, or say bad things about Susie to Nancy or vice versa. Why? First, this isn't what the Bible says to do. Secondly, it isn't how mature women act. Finally, too many times, I've seen Nancy and Susie reconcile and then turn on the person who got in the middle.

Sorry, but the Bible gives clear direction for how we are to respond when people offend us. It isn't drama, it isn't spreading rumors, and it certainly isn't gossip. In fact, the Bible is clear that gossip destroys and tears down. As Christians, we are called to build up and bring healing.

If you want to have a peaceful life, then two things to avoid are gossip and getting in the middle of other people's arguments. Instead, we need to act as peacemakers and redirect women toward applying Biblical principles to their lives and their relationships.

5. Social Media

Let me start by saying that I love social media. It's how I connect with many of my friends who live far away, and it's a vital tool in my ministry. The potential to use social media for good is limitless. Unfortunately, the pendulum can also swing the other way, and social media can be a tool of destruction and drama.

Whenever social media begins to give me a negative outlook, I've learned to set up boundaries and regain my

I Don't Do Drama

peace. Several of these boundaries include:

- A resolve that I will not participate in online arguments.

- I don't tolerate arguments on my posts—I delete argumentative comments.

- I "unfollow" those who constantly post things that steal my peace, create arguments, or are overly dramatic.

- When the drama gets too be too much, I put my phone away for a while. It may be hours or days, but I will not allow social media to steal my peace or add unnecessary drama to my life.

These steps, along with the other boundaries that I've shared, have made a tremendous difference in my life. However, it all started when I made the conscious decision that I did not want to be a forty-something drama queen. I want to be a woman who walks in peace.

The only way that I know how to do this is to determine inside of my heart and mind that whenever drama sends an invite to its party, I am not going to RSVP. Over and over again, as I've made this choice, I've found that I prefer joy over panic, calm over chaos, and peace over drama.

Because while drama may be fun for teenage girls, it is the thief of joy and peace in adult women. If you want to enjoy your life more, choose to avoid unnecessary drama.

Trust me; you'll be so glad you did.

Write in your journal how these verses apply to this chapter's topic:

"You will keep in perfect peace all who trust in you, all whose thoughts are fixed on you!" (Isaiah 26:3, NLT)

"I have told you all this so that you may have peace in me. Here on earth you will have many trials and sorrows. But take heart, because I have overcome the world." (John 16:33, NLT)

"Wrongdoers eagerly listen to gossip; liars pay close attention to slander." (Proverbs 17:4, NLT)

"If another believer sins against you, go privately and point out the offense. If the other person listens and confesses it, you have won that person back.

But if you are unsuccessful, take one or two others with you and go back again, so that everything you say may be confirmed by two or three witnesses.

If the person still refuses to listen, take your case to the church. Then if he or she won't accept the church's decision, treat that person as a pagan or a corrupt tax collector." (Matthew 18:15-17, NLT)

I Don't Do Drama

"Since God has so generously let us in on what he is doing, we're not about to throw up our hands and walk off the job just because we run into occasional hard times.

We refuse to wear masks and play games.

We don't maneuver and manipulate behind the scenes.

And we don't twist God's Word to suit ourselves.

Rather, we keep everything we do and say out in the open, the whole truth on display, so that those who want to can see and judge for themselves in the presence of God." (2 Corinthians 4:1-4, MSG)

Chapter 9

Yesterday Does Not Determine Tomorrow

"No matter what happened in your past, it doesn't have to control your future. Do whatever it takes to overcome your past and gain freedom."

I was in my mid-thirties when I started watching a show about a single mother and her teenage daughter. Almost immediately, I was a fan. I loved the witty banter between them, the independent spirit of the mom, and the unique way she saw the adventurous side of almost anything. Because I had some issues with my Dad, I could identify with her struggles with her parents. Talk about a strained relationship!

Through the course of the series, she and her parents went from not speaking to each other, through a roller coaster of working through their past, and attempting to move forward into a healthier place. At this time in my life, I could easily identify. Honestly, I found her ability to overcome her past and move forward both realistic and inspiring. When the series ended, the leading lady was no longer in the same place as when the series began. She'd worked through many of the issues in her past, found a level of forgiveness and understanding toward her parents, and carved out a very nice life.

Then a few years later, a streaming service decided to make a reboot. I HATED IT. Why?

Beyond the fact that it was way too liberal for my preferences, I hated it because I didn't want to see a woman in her fifties regressing and still struggling to overcome the same issues that bogged her down in her thirties. That is just too sad. Instead, I wanted to see growth, maturity, and a woman who had finally put her past behind her and was enjoying the freedom to live her life in the present with plans for a bright future.

While the writers of the series may not have felt that was realistic from a secular point of view, as a Christian, I do not believe that it has to be this way for women of God. In fact, I know it doesn't have to be this way because I've experienced a different scenario in my own life.

You see, I, too, entered into my twenties and thirties with a lot of baggage from my past. I had just graduated from college when we found out that everything my Dad told us about his family, his childhood, and even much of his life

Yesterday Does Not Determine Tomorrow

with us had been a lie. This revelation led our whole family down a path of seeing many lies uncovered, discovering how my Dad had abused each of us in different ways, and how his lies and wrong choices had twisted our thinking.

I spent much of my late twenties and early thirties on what I call my journey to healing. I was overcoming the issues in my life created in the past. Personally, and as part of a family, we spent years working through problems, going to counseling, and following the principles laid out in the Bible to find inner healing.

No, it was not a simple process—far too detailed to completely share in one chapter of a devotional book. It was more of a journey. That's why I wrote a whole book, *"Finding Healing,"* about it. If you are looking for an open, honest account of how to use Biblical principles to find healing in your own life, I highly recommend you read it.

Why? Because today I stand as a testimony that all of the effort—every hour, every dime, every tear, every trip to the counselor—that you put into overcoming your past is worth it for the freedom and victory you'll gain. Whether your issues came from something that happened to you or the poor choices that you made, your future does not have to be controlled by your past. There is hope for healing, freedom, and a new way of living life through Jesus Christ.

Isaiah 53:4 says that when Jesus came to die on the cross, *"He was hurt for our wrong-doing. He was crushed for our sins. He was punished so we would have peace. He was beaten so we would be healed." (NLT)*

This healing isn't just for our physical bodies, but it includes healing in our minds, our emotions, and our spirits. I believe that it is God's will that all of His sons and daughters experience this level of healing. Salvation isn't just a ticket out of Hell and into Heaven. Jesus' sacrifice brings each of us the healing that we need to overcome every area of our past that left us damaged.

With all of my heart, I believe that there is nothing the Heavenly Father wants more than to heal the damage in your soul. One by one, He wants to heal your memories, heal the damage done to your heart, and help you overcome your past. He wants you to become the woman He created you to be. However, He cannot begin this process until you permit Him.

This is where each of us faces a choice.

Do you want to continue living in the pain of the past, or do you want to be free?

Are you willing to face the past and bury it once and for all so that it stops damaging your future?

Will you allow God the time necessary to take you through this process, believing that everything He does is for your good?

I think the real question each us has to answer is:

"How long do we want to let the pain from our past control us?"

Do we want to carry it into our thirties, our forties, our fifties? Do we want to be the old woman at the nursing home

Yesterday Does Not Determine Tomorrow

still caught in the same heartaches she struggled with as a teenager? Do we want to stay trapped in the pain of our memories, carry the burden of unforgiveness, and let the entire story of our lives be tainted by something that happened years ago?

I do not.

The good news is that we don't need to live out this scenario because the choice lies with each of us. Instead, today, right now, each of us can decide that we are going to take a cue from the movie *Frozen* and begin to *"let it go."*

Today is a great day to say *"goodbye"* to our past and determine that we are going to do whatever it takes to confront our problems, to work through them, and to apply the Biblical principles of Finding Healing to our lives.

I promise you that your future self who will be walking in freedom and living a life of victory will thank you for it.

Ageless Truths

Write in your journal how these verses apply to this chapter's topic:

"Jesus heard about it and spoke up, 'Who needs a doctor: the healthy or the sick? I'm here inviting outsiders, not insiders—an invitation to a changed life, changed inside and out.'" (Luke 5:31-32, the Message)

"The Spirit of God, the Master, is on me because God anointed me. He sent me to preach good news to the poor, heal the heartbroken, Announce freedom to all captives, pardon all prisoners." (Isaiah 61:1, the Message)

"The robber comes only to steal and to kill and to destroy. I came so they might have life, a great full life." (John 10:10, NLT)

"For if a man belongs to Christ, he is a new person. The old life is gone. New life has begun." (2 Corinthians 5:17, NLT)

Chapter 10

Overcoming Criticism

"Embrace advice, but stay away from pointless criticism."

It was around 8 p.m. when my phone rang. As soon as I saw who was calling, I cringed. Besides the fact that I didn't want to interrupt the movie I was watching (one of my favorite chick flicks), I did not want to have the conversation that waited on the other side of the line.

I'd had it too many times before.

The conversation starts pleasantly enough. *"Hi. How are you doing? What's new with you?"* Of course, my answers to these questions only lead to a recitation of how busy, how successful, and how vital my friend is to the world.

Then, it begins.

The comparison. The condescending attitude. The criticism.

The last time we talked, she used the word *"just"* to describe my life so many times that I began to wonder if I do anything of any value for anyone at all. It wasn't until I received an encouraging note from another friend that I could shake off the feeling of total inadequacy. If this were just a one-time thing, perhaps I'd have answered the phone, but this has been a pattern in this relationship for the past twenty years.

That's why I let the call roll to voicemail.

I was proud of my self for rejecting it. For me, it showed growth. It showed that I respected myself enough to say *"enough," "no more," "this pattern has to end."*

As I continued watching my movie, I was quite proud that when the voice of criticism tried to make a house call, I didn't answer the phone. I am learning as I mature that genuine advice given by a loving friend will change your life and prove invaluable. Pointless criticism from someone who wants to tear you down is merely destructive. I don't need it. When they call, I'm not picking up the phone.

You must understand the first line in that statement. I genuinely believe that a loving friend's genuine advice will change your life and prove invaluable. The more I mature, the more I appreciate the people in my life who provide godly advice. Over the past decade, I have gone out of my way, seeking people willing to share their wisdom. I truly believe that:

Overcoming Criticism

> *"The way of fools seems right to them, but the wise listen to advice."* (Proverbs 12:15, NIV)

> *"Without good direction, people lose their way; the more wise counsel you follow, the better your chances."* (Proverbs 11:14, MSG)

> *"Listen to advice and accept discipline, and at the end you will be counted among the wise."* (Proverbs 19:20, NIV)

Years ago, I determined in my heart that I wanted to be a woman who was willing to learn from others. Whether it be how to improve my character, how to function in ministry, how to have better relationships, or how to care for my home, I recognize that I don't know what I don't know. The best way to improve myself and my skills are to be willing to learn from other people.

Part of that has involved being open to correction. When it came time for my brother and me to choose the people who would be on our ministry's board of directors and serve as our advisors, we looked for people with strong opinions. We didn't want people who said *"yes"* to everything or stroked our egos. We knew that we didn't need to hear we did everything right. Instead, we asked people who would be bluntly honest with us, who would push us to do more, reach further, try harder.

Over the years, they have not failed us! One of my favorite stories is the time when one of my mentors called me on the phone to tell me that the ministry videos I was posting on Facebook were terrible. She said I either needed to up my game and improve the quality of the videos or stop making them because they were hurting the ministry. (Yep, she had no problem being honest.)

But here's where she is different from my friend who wants to criticize. When my mentor called to correct me, she didn't just point out problems. Instead, she took the time to make a list of the problematic things in the videos and gave suggestions for how I could fix it. She was right! As I began implementing her recommendations, the quality of our video production improved dramatically. People even started asking how they could learn to do them similarly!

That is the value of accepting advice! Even though it may sting at the moment, in the end, it produces good fruit in your life. It reminds me of Proverbs 27:6, which says, **"Wounds from a friend can be trusted, but an enemy multiplies kisses." (NIV)**

This is why I believe that one of the best decisions a woman can make is to be open to godly advice and correction.

Criticism, on the other hand, is a different matter entirely. While *"correction"* is constructive, *"criticism"* is destructive. It doesn't seek to build you up; it only desires to tear you down and keep you down.

Correction brings healing; criticism causes unnecessary pain.

Correction provides hope; criticism makes you feel hopeless.

Overcoming Criticism

Correction wants to see you improve, do better, grow stronger, reach for the stars, and be the best you can be. Criticism, on the other hand, reminds you that you'll never be good enough, that you are too weak, too small, and utterly incapable of reaching the standard of the one who is offering the criticism.

Most importantly, correction comes from God; criticism comes from the enemy, Satan.

It is so vital that as godly women, we learn to discern the difference between correction and criticism so that we can embrace one and reject the other. Just like we judge the quality of the food we put into our bodies, we need to learn to judge the quality of the words that we allow to take up residence in our hearts and spirits.

As I shared in the beginning, there was a time when I let a friend's critical words take residence in my spirit. For almost two weeks, I questioned my value, my life choices, and my purpose because she said that I was *"just"* assisting on a project and had that cute little blog. I allowed her condescending, critical words to determine how I felt about myself.

Sadly, too many women allow the cruel, critical words of another to reside in their spirit for even longer. Carrying the words of a critical parent, teacher, spouse, or boss with them for ten, twenty, thirty, or more years, they have let criticism steal their life, joy, and true self-worth. This is not God's will for their lives.

Instead, God wants to release you from the burden of

unjust criticism. He wants to show you that their words were lies, and He wants to set you free completely.

Then, He wants to teach you to differentiate between honest, loving, godly correction, and criticism. Through the power of the Holy Spirit, He wants you to learn to embrace correction and turn a deaf ear to criticism.

Over the years, this is what He has been teaching me. After years of working through the Biblical steps to Finding Healing, I have experienced emotional and mental healing from criticism I carried with me for far too long. Through this process, I've also learned the difference between godly counsel and criticism.

As I've grown older, I've learned that I need to respect myself enough to take a stand when it comes to criticism. I've learned that I can choose whether I allow it to enter my heart, my spirit, and even my ears. That's why I didn't answer the phone that night. I was protecting my heart, protecting my mind, and choosing what I would allow into my spirit.

I only wish I had done it sooner.

Proverbs 4:23 says, **"Keep vigilant watch over your heart; that's where life starts." (The Message)**

One way to do this is by choosing to embrace godly counsel while rejecting unnecessary criticism. Whenever criticism calls, send it to voicemail. Then maybe delete the voicemail. You don't need to hear it.

Overcoming Criticism

Write in your journal how these verses apply to this chapter's topic:

"The way of fools seems right to them, but the wise listen to advice." (Proverbs 12:15, NIV)

"Without good direction, people lose their way; the more wise counsel you follow, the better your chances." (Proverbs 11:14, MSG)

"Listen to advice and accept discipline, and at the end you will be counted among the wise." (Proverbs 19:20, NIV)

"Wounds from a friend can be trusted, but an enemy multiplies kisses." (Proverbs 27:6, NIV)

"Keep vigilant watch over your heart; that's where life starts." (Proverbs 4:23, MSG)

Chapter 11

Who Made You the Boss?

"In my forties, I learned to be myself and let others be themselves, too."

I'd just turned forty when our ministry's advisory board insisted that I attend a retreat for women in ministry. Yes, I said, *"insisted"* because I did not want to go. I only went because they said I should. Even though they assured me that I would enjoy it and it would be good for me, heading into the weekend, I was nervous.

You see, the issue was that even though this retreat had recently been renamed the *"Women in Ministry Retreat,"* most people were still affectionately calling it the *"Pastor's Wives Retreat."* Being single, I could not imagine how awkward I would feel as the minority in the crowd. (By minority, I mean I was the only unmarried woman there.)

As I walked into the campground, I moved from nervous to downright scared. I thought, *"What if the other women don't like me? What if they point out that I don't belong? What if they don't say it to my face, but talk about me behind my back?"* Looking back now, I see that my insecurities were feeding my fear. Still working to overcome the idea that being single made me less valuable than a married woman, I assumed everyone else felt that way.

I was only there a few hours when I called my brother, who'd dropped me off at the retreat, and asked him to come back so I could go home. Fortunately, he said he was caught in traffic and couldn't possibly be there for several hours. I had to calm down and at least make it through the evening service. Inevitably, the traffic was a good thing because it forced me to stay at the event. As the evening went on and I met more people, my fears began to go away. Over the next few days, I found that my fears were completely unfounded.

Rather than rejection and ridicule, I found friends. In the end, I was the only one worried about the fact that I was single. All of the women I met were very friendly and kind, and we had a lot in common. Many of these friendships have grown since the retreat and expanded into robust, reliable friendships. They've become the women I text when I have a funny story and the ones I call when I need prayer. They are a blessing in my life, and I hope I've been the same in their lives.

Yet, looking back, these friendships almost didn't happen because I was afraid to step out of my comfort zone and let other people out of the little boxes I built based on my feelings of inadequacy. My insecurities were causing me to build walls, and my assumptions and preconceived ideas kept me in prison. It wasn't until my board forced me into a situation where I had to let my walls down that I saw the ridiculousness of my preconceived ideas.

One thing I learned that weekend is that if I want people to accept me and God's unique plan for my life, I need to extend the same courtesy to them. When we let each other out of the *"little boxes"* of how people should be, we learn that variety is the spice of life. We can enjoy the freedom to be ourselves and enjoy the differences that another person's perspective brings to life.

Putting this truth into action has changed my life. When I started making friends with people who were different from me—different ages, marital statuses, and career goals—my life became fuller.

It's like a salad—who wants to eat just lettuce every day?

Isn't a salad much more enjoyable when you add some tomatoes, cucumbers, carrots, a little cheese, some broccoli, and some spicy dressing?

The same thing is true in life. God didn't create us to all be the same. The best thing we can do for ourselves and each other is to accept this truth.

Embrace the differences.

See how we can complement each other rather than criticize.

Learn to be yourself and let other people be themselves, also. It's the only way everyone can meet their full potential—you, me, and the church at large.

As it says in 1 Corinthians 12, God made us all differently. He's given us all a unique story, an individual purpose, and a distinct calling to fulfill. Just as each one of us has a responsibility to seek and pursue God's purpose for our lives, we need to allow others to do the same.

Yet I find it interesting right after Paul talks about our differences; he talks about the need for us to love one another. He reminds us that *"Love is patient, love is kind. It does not envy, it does not boast, it is not proud. It does not dishonor others, it is not self-seeking, it is not easily angered, it keeps no record of wrongs. Love does not delight in evil but rejoices with the truth. It always protects, always trusts, always hopes, always perseveres" (I Corinthians 13:4-7, NIV)*. More important than all of the things that we do, the most important thing is how we treat each other—even if we are different.

When God leads another woman to do something differently, it is not your job to judge or criticize. Instead, we should encourage and support each other to follow Jesus wholeheartedly. As we do this, we are building up others, and we are also building up the kingdom of God.

Over the years, as I've applied the principle of being myself and letting other people be themselves, I have found friends in some of the most unexpected places. I have friends who are younger and older than me, friends who are married and single, friends with and without kids, and even friends who disagree with me or are called to walk a path that I wouldn't have chosen. Yet, as we've allowed each other to be ourselves and follow the unique plan that God has for each of our lives, we've found that the things we have in common are far greater than the things that might divide. They make my life richer and fuller by merely being a part of it.

So here's my advice: stop putting people in boxes.

Stop trying to play God and determine who everyone should be and what they should do.

Instead, work on overcoming your insecurities and the issues that cause you to build walls around your heart. Ask the Holy Spirit if there are any assumptions or preconceived ideas that keep you from accepting the way God is leading others.

As it says in Matthew 7:3-5, ***"Why do you look at the speck of sawdust in your brother's eye and pay no attention to the plank in your own eye? How can you say to your brother, 'Let me take the speck out of your eye,' when all the time there is a plank in your own eye? You hypocrite, first take the plank out of your own eye, and then you will see clearly to remove the speck from your brother's eye."***

Go back just a few verses, and we read that it is not our job to sit as judge over another person's life and choices. (Matthew 7:1-2) Of course, this doesn't mean that we shouldn't help another woman if she is falling into sin. Galatians 6:1-3 tells us we should try to help others in this situation. However, these verses only apply when someone is doing something morally wrong that will affect their eternal destiny, not when someone takes a different approach than we would have chosen or preferred. In my years of walking with Jesus, I've found most are far more likely to judge someone over a small disagreement than to take the risk and confront someone about sin in their lives. Too many women are more likely to talk about someone to their friends than to actually go to a friend in love and try to help. These actions are wrong, and they must stop.

Instead, we all need to remember the words of Jesus when He said, **"So in everything, do to others what you would have them do to you" (Matthew 7:12, NIV).** Just as we want others to allow us the freedom to be who God made us and follow God's unique path for our lives, so we need to let others do the same. Along the way, we need to learn to enjoy the differences realizing that God didn't make us all the same. Instead, He designed us all differently so that we could complement and complete each other as we all work toward the greater good of advancing His kingdom.

Along the way, we need to learn to enjoy the differences. Who knows if someone else's variety isn't just the thing you need to spice up your life and bring out the best in you? I know that's what happened for me as I learned not just to be myself, but also to let others be themselves. Life became much fuller, richer, and honestly, a lot more fun.

Who Made You the Boss?

Write in your journal how these verses apply to this chapter's topic:

"Do not judge, or you too will be judged. For in the same way you judge others, you will be judged, and with the measure you use, it will be measured to you." (Matthew 7:1-2, NIV)

"Why do you look at the speck of sawdust in your brother's eye and pay no attention to the plank in your own eye? How can you say to your brother, 'Let me take the speck out of your eye,' when all the time there is a plank in your own eye? You hypocrite, first take the plank out of your own eye, and then you will see clearly to remove the speck from your brother's eye." (Matthew 7:3-5, NIV)

"So in everything, do to others what you would have them do to you." (Matthew 7:12, NIV)

"Now you are the body of Christ, and each one of you is a part of it.

And God has placed in the church first of all apostles, second prophets, third teachers, then miracles, then gifts of healing, of helping, of guidance, and of different kinds of tongues.

Are all apostles? Are all prophets? Are all teachers? Do all work miracles? Do all have gifts of healing? Do all speak in tongues? Do all interpret?

Now eagerly desire the greater gifts. And yet I will show you the most excellent way." (1 Corinthians 12:27-31, NIV)

"And now these three remain: faith, hope and love. But the greatest of these is love." (1 Corinthians 13:13, NIV)

Chapter 12

Who Wouldn't Like Me?

"Not everyone is going to like you, understand you, or agree with you. It's okay. You are called to follow Jesus, not popular opinion."

So here's an interesting fact: I don't like steak. It doesn't matter if it's a juicy porterhouse, a grilled t-bone, or even filet mignon, I'm not a fan.

Yes, I know, many people love steak. They think it is the best meal in the world and spend big money to enjoy it at a restaurant. It's just not my thing. I don't get the fascination.

I know this may be difficult for all of the steak lovers to understand. I feel the same way about my friend, who doesn't like chocolate. To me, this is incomprehensible. Since I'm pretty sure chocolate is God's gift to women to make up for fluctuating hormones, I can't imagine not loving it. Still, my friend isn't a fan.

Another thing I'm not crazy about is blue jeans. Honesty, I dread every time I'm forced to wear them. Who thinks they are comfortable? Yes, I know, almost everyone on the planet except me. Still, they aren't my style.

At this point, you might be thinking, *"Okay, these are odd facts, but what's the point?"*

Well, I'm getting to it. Here it is:

Just because I don't like steak or blue jeans or my friend doesn't like chocolate doesn't take away the fact that these are still amazing products that most people love and can't imagine life without. Just because they aren't my taste or your taste doesn't diminish their value.

The same thing is true of people.

Whether you've realized it yet or not in your life, there are going to be people who don't like you. (Shocking, isn't it?) Still, it happens to us all. Some people's personalities will not be compatible with your personality. Others just won't find you their cup of tea.

This is perfectly alright.

It doesn't diminish your value.

It doesn't mean there is something wrong with you.

Just like my distaste for steak and blue jeans doesn't

Who Wouldn't Like Me?

change the fact that they are a popular favorite of millions of other people, your worth is not changed by the fact that one person doesn't like you. It just means that they aren't "your people."

Let's be honest: we all have *"our people"*—the people you meet and instantly you know that you are kindred spirits. Other people "grow on you" over time. Even though it may not have been love at first sight, as you got to know them, it turned out you were kindred spirits after all. Then there are those people that we just don't like. We're not compatible. No matter how much time you spend with them, you just don't *"click."* It doesn't mean there's something wrong with you or with them. They just aren't "your people".

One of the things many women learn as they mature is that this is totally normal. It's no big deal. Some people are going to like you, and some just aren't. When this happens, the best thing to do is shrug it off. Don't let it change how you feel about yourself or your value. Just accept that you aren't compatible and move on living your life with the many people who do love you.

Because as the popular saying goes: *"You aren't pizza, not everyone is going to like you."* The earlier in life you accept this lesson, the better.

For some women, this lesson comes quite easily. However, if you are like me, and fall into the category of the *"people-pleaser,"* then accepting this truth can be a little bit more of a struggle. For too much of my early life, instead of simply accepting that someone didn't like me and moving on,

I determined that I would do what I needed to do to make them like me.

For example:

Don't think I'm *"fun"* enough? Think I'm too serious? Well, watch how fun I can be as I turn myself into a silly clown that even I don't like to try to make you like me!

Don't think we have anything in common? Wait! I'll pretend to like everything you like so that we can be best buddies! Do you like me now?

Think my opinions are too strong? I can quiet them. I'll just agree with you about everything.

These were just a few of the ways that I would change myself so that people would like me, approve of me, and, most importantly, validate my self-worth.

Besides being super agreeable, I also tried being super helpful.

Need a volunteer to do the job no one else wants to do? I'm your gal.

Can I make your life easier? That will make you like me, right?

Yet, looking back, all of this work and all of the changes that I made didn't really change people's minds. Sure, they'd accept the help, but we didn't become friends because we just weren't compatible. In the end, all of my work, all my changing, all of the energy and effort that I put into trying to make them like me was just a waste. It wasn't their fault, and it wasn't mine. We either genuinely didn't have anything in common, had very different personalities, or God just didn't intend for us to be a part of each other's lives.

I had to learn to accept that this was alright. It was perfectly normal....just a part of life. It didn't make me less valuable as a person. It didn't mean I was unlovable. Honestly, it was no reflection on me at all. Some people will love you, some people will like you, and others just won't. The day that I learned to accept this truth and stop wasting my energy trying to please people and make everyone like me was one of the most liberating days of my life.

Even more liberating was the day when I decided that no matter what, I was going to be myself. If someone didn't like me, oh well, it was their loss.

I remember the day I tried this attitude out on one of my close friends. We were having a discussion, and I disagreed with her about something. Only those who have truly struggled with an addiction to pleasing people will understand how hard it was to admit, *"I actually don't like that."* I remember being so scared that she'd be offended. What if she got her knickers in a knot and never wanted to talk to me again?

Still, I knew I had to speak up. The Holy Spirit had been working overtime on my heart to help me overcome people-pleasing and be my authentic, genuine self. Now it was time to put what I'd been learning into practice no matter what the result.

So I took a deep breath and told the truth—I didn't like what she liked.

Her response, *"Really? Wow, I can't imagine."* Then she laughed and moved on with the conversation.

Even though I'm sure that my friend doesn't remember that day or conversation at all, it left a big impression with me. It showed me that true friends don't try to change you. They may challenge you or confront you when you are truly wrong, but they aren't trying to give you a personality makeover. Real friends love you just the way you are—you don't have to work for it.

It also gave me the confidence to step out and continue being myself, expressing my opinions, showing my truly authentic side in even more relationships. Time and again, I saw that with *"my people,"* it was safe to completely be myself. There was no need to hide, work to gain love and approval, or be anything less than who God made me.

On the flip side, time has taught me that no matter how hard you work or change, you can't make someone like you. When you run into those rare people who simply aren't *"your people,"* you can't let it bother you. You need to simply accept that it wasn't meant to be, shrug it off, and move on with your life.

Over the years, as I've continued to mature and overcome my struggle with people-pleasing, I've finally settled into the truth that people don't determine your value, God does. As long as you are following Him and becoming the woman that He wants you to be, it doesn't matter who else approves. As

Who Wouldn't Like Me?

Paul says in Galatians 1:10, *"Am I now trying to win the approval of human beings, or of God? Or am I trying to please people? If I were still trying to please people, I would not be a servant of Christ."*

In this Scripture, we see that we are not called to live for the approval of people. Our goal in life should be to please God. As we do this, we can trust that He will bring people into our lives who will love us, accept us, and walk with us as we all seek to pursue God's will for our lives. Personally, I've seen this time and again, as God has brought people into my life who have become dear friends, strong support systems, and true companions. Around these people I don't have to pretend to be anything I'm not, I just get to be me as I let them be them. That's the way a healthy friendship should be.

As I seek to live my life for God's approval, I learn that my value is determined by Him, not people's opinions. This makes it so much easier to retain my peace when someone doesn't like me. Rather than stressing over why they don't like me, what's wrong with me, or why aren't I good enough to be their friend I can simply shrug it off and think, *"We're just not compatible…it's okay…I don't like everyone either."*

Speaking of peace, I cannot tell you the peace it has brought into my life since I have overcome my struggle with pleasing people. Seriously, that is an exhausting burden to carry! It is so much easier to simply live your life to please God and accept the fact that not everyone is going to like you, understand you, or agree with you. It's okay. You are called to follow Jesus, not popular opinion.

Just like steak, chocolate, and blue jeans, one person's preferences don't diminish the fact that you are loved, you are valuable, and you truly are awesome.

Write in your journal how these verses apply to this chapter's topic:

"We are not trying to please people but God, who tests our hearts." (1 Thessalonians 2:4b, NLT)

"Am I now trying to win the approval of human beings, or of God? Or am I trying to please people? If I were still trying to please people, I would not be a servant of Christ." (Galatians 1:10, NLT)

"Yet at the same time many even among the leaders believed in him. But because of the Pharisees they would not openly acknowledge their faith for fear they would be put out of the synagogue; for they loved human praise more than praise from God." (John 12:42-43, NIV)

Chapter 13

Change of Plans

"There comes the point in life where you have to stop grieving the life you thought you'd have and embrace the life God has given you."

Do you remember being eighteen? Bright-eyed and full of plans for the future, we all had an idea of what our lives would look like. For most girls in my generation, that meant dreaming of the man they would marry, planning an elaborate over-the-top wedding as we saw in *"Father of the Bride,"* and dreaming of how we could have it all as we juggled family and career.

We all enter into adulthood with a picture of what our lives will be. Yet, most of us eventually find out that God's plan for our lives rarely follows our script. For some, the alterations are more dramatic. Others may find that God allowed their lives to follow the path they imagined, but it wasn't the way they thought it would be.

Either way, the result can lead to disappointment and grief. If we aren't careful, we can fall into the trap of grieving our lives away over the way things should have been. This is not God's will for His girls.

This is a lesson I had to learn in my own life. Growing up, I had a plan for my life. I imagined myself married, a mother, and serving alongside my husband in ministry. I planned to move out of the tiny town where I grew up—maybe even move to the city. According to my plan, by this time in my life, I should be a grandmother, an empty-nester preparing to start my second act. With my kids out and on their own, I'd be free to serve full time in ministry (my true dream and calling since I was seven years old).

As many of you know, things did not turn out the way I planned. Now in my mid-forties, I have never been married, I have no children, and instead of ministering with a husband, I am one-half of a brother-sister team. I still live in the small town where I grew up. I actually live in the same house. Last summer, we converted our garage into office space for our ministry (which makes me assume I'll be here for a while).

In short, nothing in my life turned out the way I imagined when I was eighteen. I have to confess that I spent many years grieving the disappointment. I wondered, *"How could God let my life turn out this way? Why did He make me walk such a difficult road?"* Many times I questioned if I took a wrong path and missed God's will for my life. Other times I wondered if God had a plan at all. Over the years, I've cried, I've prayed, I've gotten angry and thrown temper tantrums, and deeply grieved the loss of my plans. So believe me when I say that I understand the pain some women feel as they realize that the plans they had for their lives will not happen.

However, over the years, I've also learned another very important lesson: although there is a time for grieving the death of a dream, there is also a time when the grieving must end.

As Solomon says in Ecclesiastes 3:4, there is a *"time to weep and a time to laugh, a time to mourn and a time to dance."*

What I've learned is that no matter how different God's plan for your life is then you thought it would be, there must come the point when you surrender your plans and submit to God's plan. There is absolutely no benefit to spending your life like an angry, spoiled child punishing the world because you didn't get your own way. I've seen too many women live this way, and it just isn't good. They are miserable, and everyone around them is miserable. After they've wasted their lives swimming in self-pity and a victim mentality, they end up bitter, angry old women. I made a decision a long time ago that this was absolutely not who I wanted to be.

Instead, as I entered my thirties, I decided that I was going to take a different path. I forced myself to put aside my disappointment and embrace a different attitude of loving the life God chose to give me. As I chose to *"put on"* a new attitude, I came to a few realizations that helped my attitude genuinely change.

The first thing I realized was that **God knew more than I did.**

I get it; sometimes, this is hard to admit. I mean, we spend so much time focusing on our plans that we think they must be perfect. After all, who knows us better than we know ourselves?

Well, God does.

One thing I had to accept was that the plan I had for my life would not have turned out as *"happily-ever-after"* as I thought it would. God knew this even though I didn't.

You see, what God saw that I didn't was that at twenty years old, there were many broken places in my heart that needed to be healed and so many parts of my mind that needed to be renewed. Before I could even think of having a healthy relationship or ministering to anyone, I needed to find out about my Dad's secrets, to face the abuse I grew up with, and to learn that God doesn't view women through eyes of hate as my Dad did. Even though at the time, I didn't see or even know about these issues, God did. Ultimately, the plan that I hated to bring me back home so I could face these problems was exactly what I needed.

Even though I couldn't see past my *"ride-off-into-the-sunset"* fantasy, God could. He knew that had my life followed my plan; it would not have been a dream come true.

Change Of Plans

Today, I know beyond a shadow of a doubt that I'd either be divorced or in an abusive marriage like my parents. I'd never be in ministry. These aren't pretty facts, but they are facts that God knew. He loved me enough to say, *"Let's take a different path than you planned."*

Even though at the time, I thought that coming back home after college as a single woman with no job was the cruelest thing God could have done, I now see His kindness. He knew what I didn't know, and He saved me a world of heartache. His plan to heal my heart was the best thing that ever happened to me, even though it wasn't what I wanted.

Perhaps it was realizing this that helped me realize that **God's plans are always better than our plans.**

> *"For my thoughts are not your thoughts, neither are your ways my ways," declares the Lord. "As the heavens are higher than the earth, so are my ways higher than your ways and my thoughts than your thoughts." (Isaiah 55:8-9, NIV)*

I know, I know, it's one thing to quote this verse. It's another thing to truly believe it. Yet, I can testify in my own life that this is completely true. Looking back on my life, I can see that the plan I had for my life was created by a silly, naive girl who knew very little about life. On the other hand, God's plans were created by the same One Who created the world, designed the solar system, formed the human body, and orchestrated all of history. How ridiculous to think that I could even dare to tell such Genius how things should be!!

Without a doubt, it was when I stopped grieving my

plans and finally buried them, that I was able to begin appreciating the kindness, the love, and the intricateness of God's plan for my life. When I finally got over the fact that His plans were different than mine, I could finally embrace how much better His plans were. Rather than grieving my lost plans, I could fully embrace God's amazing plan and purpose for my life.

The older I get, the more I realize that even though life didn't turn out the way I planned, it doesn't matter. Those plans were made by a silly girl who didn't know anything. It's time to let her dreams go and walk in God's plans and purpose for my life.

As I've chosen this path, I can say without a doubt that God's plans have not only been different, but they have been bigger and better than anything I could imagine.

For instance, as I write this last line, my mind was drawn back to a warm evening in May in 2015. Dressed in a black suit, I stood at the altar at GT Church in West Lawn, PA, and received my ordination as an Assembly of God minister. It was one of the happiest nights of my life. Alongside my brother, surrounded by friends who have become like family, I remember crying tears of joy. It was an absolute dream come true. Yet, it was a part of God's plan that I seriously never imagined would happen.

Quite frankly, at eighteen years old, I didn't believe it was God's will for a woman to be ordained. Still living in the bondage of my Dad's abusive ideas toward women, I was convinced that the only way a woman could serve in ministry

Change Of Plans

was under her husband. I clearly remember sitting on the chapel steps at the University of Valley Forge, telling my best friend and fellow ministry major, *"No, I'll never get ordained. I don't believe it's right for women."*

It seriously wasn't part of my plan. And yet....

After years of God working on my heart, healing me, restoring my mind, and teaching me to see myself through His eyes, on that May evening, I experienced something that eighteen-year-old girl thought was impossible. As I remembered all of the tears that I shed thinking, "God doesn't have a plan. God won't let me minister because I'm not married. Why doesn't God want me anymore? Why is my life taking such a strange direction?" so many of those tears were turned to joy.

Over the years, as God has continued to lead me through doors that were above and beyond anything I could have imagined, anything I even thought women were allowed to do in God's kingdom, I have learned that God's plans are truly better than my own.

Over the years I've learned that true fulfillment and purpose are found when we give up our plans and ideas of how things should be, bury them at the foot of the cross, walk away from our grief, and into the bright future that God has for us.

So yes, have your cry over how things didn't turn out the way you want. Take your grief to God and offer your disappointment as a sacrifice.

But then let it at the altar.

Abandon it and choose that from this day forward, you will not live in grief, but instead, you will embrace all that God has for you.

It's time.

Write in your journal how these verses apply to this chapter's topic:

"When the Lord restored the fortunes of Zion, we were like those who dreamed. Our mouths were filled with laughter, our tongues with songs of joy.

Then it was said among the nations, "The Lord has done great things for them."

The Lord has done great things for us, and we are filled with joy.

Restore our fortunes, Lord, like streams in the Negev.

Those who sow with tears will reap with songs of joy. Those who go out weeping, carrying seed to sow will return with songs of joy, carrying sheaves with them." (Psalm 126, NIV)

"Now to him who is able to do immeasurably more than all we ask or imagine, according to his power that is at work within

us, to him be glory in the church and in Christ Jesus throughout all generations, for ever and ever! Amen." (Ephesians 3:20-21 NIV)

"'For my thoughts are not your thoughts, neither are your ways my ways,' declares the Lord. 'As the heavens are higher than the earth, so are my ways higher than your ways and my thoughts than your thoughts.'" (Isaiah 55:8-9, NIV)

"A time to weep and a time to laugh, a time to mourn and a time to dance," (Ecclesiastes 3:4, NIV)

Chapter 14

The Importance of Flexibility

"There is more than one way to do something—allow the Holy Spirit to use you how He wants, where He wants, and in whatever way He wants."

Every once in awhile, I'll scroll across something on social media that completely blows my mind. It puts into perspective how completely different the world is than it was twenty-something years ago when I was in college. For instance, when I was in college:

The iPhone had yet to be invented.

Very few people even had cell phones. During my senior year, the cool kids were starting to get beepers. We made long-distance phone calls using a payphone or a *"prepaid phone card"* (the ultimate in convenience).

I didn't have a computer. Instead, I had a Brother's Word Processor that sounded like a machine gun continuously going off when it printed. (It drove my roommate crazy!)

Although technically, the internet existed, no one used it or understood what it was. (Cue the Katie Couric *"Can You Explain What Internet Is"* commercial.)

Back then, we got mail from the post office. I didn't even have an email address.

You listened to music on cassette tapes and watched movies on a VCR.

The inventors of Facebook, Twitter, and Instagram were still in elementary school.

Yep, things were different.

This probably explains why so many in my generation never imagined they would be doing many of the things they are doing today. After all, many of these tasks weren't invented! For instance, even though I dreamed of being a writer one day, I naturally assumed I'd be writing for a magazine or a newspaper. The possibility of a website or blog didn't even exist. Who would have thought that in 2020 you'd be able to self-publish a book through Amazon? Back then, *"Amazon"* referred to a rainforest in Brazil.

So what's the point besides a walk down memory lane?

The Importance of Flexibility

The point is that things change. Technology advances. Old ways of doing things are replaced with new ones. With each new invention, we learn that there is more than one way to do something. If we want to be women who fully embrace the rich, abundant life that God has for us, then we need to be open to a change in our ideas of how things should happen. Instead, we must allow the Holy Spirit to use us how He wants, where He wants, and in whatever way He wants.

Sometimes we get an idea in our head of how things have to happen. When the Holy Spirit wants to take us a different route, we balk because it doesn't fit into our plan. In my forties, I've learned to abandon this practice. Instead, I'll take whatever route is open to fulfill God's plan for my life.

For instance, one of the amazing new opportunities for God's kingdom to advance and reach people has come through Amazon's self-publishing process. So many people who would never get a contract from a traditional publisher have the opportunity to share their testimony, publish their teaching curriculums, and reach people for Jesus.

In our ministry, this has not only allowed us to publish books and Bible studies that are reaching people and provide curriculum for men's and women's groups, but it allowed us to donate books to prisoners across the country. In the last five years, we've given over 5,000 books to chaplains who are using them to lead Bible studies behind prison walls, inside of rehabilitation centers, even in homeless shelters. Over and over again, we are amazed at the testimonies we hear of books being shared until they were worn through, men and women who were encouraged and inspired through the books, and lives that were changed. It's been awesome to see God move through this part of our ministry.

Yet, had my brother or I insisted on waiting until a traditional publisher purchased our books, none of this ministry would have taken place. As we put aside our ego, the status, and the financial security that comes from a traditional publisher, we were able to fulfill this part of our calling.

Looking back on the day that we decided to begin the self-publishing process, I have to admit that it was a struggle. It was still such a new way of doing things—so different than the way I thought things should be. I remembered hearing people say that you aren't a *"real author"* until a traditional platform publishes you. Yet, we believed the Holy Spirit led us in this direction, so we took a leap of faith.

Today, I'm so glad we did. Because while this route may not be traditional, the fruit it has produced is undeniable. As demonstrated by so many of our friends who have taken the same course, the Holy Spirit is using this *"new"* avenue to help spread the Gospel and disciple Christians. The same can be said of podcasts, websites, Youtube videos, and so many new technologies! Just look at the difference that social media made in continuing to reach people during the covid-19 shutdown! By adapting methods, the work of God was able to continue!!

Over and over, we can see that sometimes God's plan for life is different from ours. Sometimes He will lead you on a different route. Other times your dreams will agree with His,

The Importance of Flexibility

but He will take you on a different path than you imagined to fulfill them.

In these instances, the best thing we can do is be flexible.

Keep an open mind to new possibilities. Perhaps God has a different road, a better path to get you where He wants you to go. When the Holy Spirit leads you in a new direction, don't ever make the mistake of saying, *"Nope. It's my way or the highway. If I can't have it exactly as I wanted it, I don't want it at all."*

News flash: Clinging to old ways of *"this is how it has to be"* can leave you waiting forever. Being open to new methods and embracing change can open doors you couldn't even imagine.

Once again, it returns to the principles of the last chapter:

We need to remember that God knows more than we do.

God's ways are better than our ways.

He not only sees what worked in the past and will work for today, but He knows what is coming and will work in the future.

When we trust Him enough to take a leap of faith and follow His direction, even if it means walking in uncharted territory, it can lead to the greatest adventure of our lives.

Who knows if the *"new thing"* God is leading you into today might not be standard practice ten or twenty years from now? You may be a trailblazer!!! How cool would that be?

Remember: throughout history, God has always called His people to embrace change. For instance, in Acts 10, God gave Peter a vision telling Him that because of the work of Christ at the cross, it was now God's will that Jews could not only eat meat that was previously unclean, but that Christians should take the Gospel to the Gentiles! This was shocking!! Against every cultural norm and tradition Peter was taught, the Holy Spirit was now leading Him in a new direction. (Acts 10:9-23)

Yet, it was this new direction that provided a way for you and me and the rest of the world to hear the Gospel, to have a relationship with God, to be forgiven of our sins, and spend eternity with God. When Peter and the other disciples followed the Holy Spirit into a new territory, God's kingdom was advanced.

Today, God wants to do the same thing in our lives. The question is, will we, like Peter, follow the Holy Spirit's lead? Will we allow Him to lead us through new doors, past the way we've always done things, and into God's plan for the future?

For me, it's an absolute *"yes!"* Like Moses, Caleb, and Abraham, I want to follow God boldly into the future and play my role in God's kingdom. Often that means embracing flexibility. Following God whenever, wherever, and in whatever way He leads. Who's with me?

The Importance of Flexibility

Write in your journal how these verses apply to this chapter's topic:

"See, I am doing a new thing! Now it springs up; do you not perceive it? I am making a way in the wilderness and streams in the wasteland." (Isaiah 43:19, NIV)

"Have I not commanded you? Be strong and courageous. Do not be afraid; do not be discouraged, for the Lord your God will be with you wherever you go." (Joshua 1:9, NIV)

"About noon the following day as they were on their journey and approaching the city, Peter went up on the roof to pray. He became hungry and wanted something to eat, and while the meal was being prepared, he fell into a trance.

He saw heaven opened and something like a large sheet being let down to earth by its four corners. It contained all kinds of four-footed animals, as well as reptiles and birds.

Then a voice told him, 'Get up, Peter. Kill and eat.'

'Surely not, Lord!' Peter replied. 'I have never eaten anything impure or unclean.'

The voice spoke to him a second time, 'Do not call anything impure that God has made clean.'

This happened three times, and immediately the sheet was taken back to heaven.

While Peter was wondering about the meaning of the vision, the men sent by Cornelius found out where Simon's house was and stopped at the gate. They called out, asking if Simon who was known as Peter was staying there.

While Peter was still thinking about the vision, the Spirit said to him, 'Simon, three men are looking for you. So get up and go downstairs. Do not hesitate to go with them, for I have sent them.'

Peter went down and said to the men, 'I'm the one you're looking for. Why have you come?'

The men replied, 'We have come from Cornelius the centurion. He is a righteous and God-fearing man, who is respected by all the Jewish people. A holy angel told him to ask you to come to his house so that he could hear what you have to say.'

Then Peter invited the men into the house to be his guests.

The next day Peter started out with them, and some of the believers from Joppa went along." (Acts 10:9-23, NIV)

Chapter 15

Hot Flashes Are Real

"Hot flashes are real and so is everything else involved with PMS and perimenopause."

Contrary to a popular sitcom where a woman was told she entered perimenopause before the first commercial, dealt with her symptoms before the second commercial, and was all cured before the show was over (never to be mentioned again in future episodes), the symptoms of perimenopause don't arrive and wrap themselves up in a half-hour. They go on and on and on. Oh, how I wish the sitcom were real! Unfortunately, it hasn't been that way in my life.

Instead, I started experiencing the symptoms of perimenopause (the season where your body goes through all of the changes that lead to actual menopause) in my early forties. At first, I didn't understand what was happening, and

I was really scared as I imagined all of the things that could be going wrong. A few months later, an older friend said, "*Everything you describe sounds like what I went through in perimenopause.*" After a talk with my doctor and a test to make sure it wasn't my thyroid, the doctor confirmed that I was entering the glorious time in life known as *"the change."* For me, it's been more like a tornado affecting every area of my life.

Some things I've learned since then is that:

The symptoms of perimenopause are very real. While hot flashes and mood swings get all the attention, there are also many other physical symptoms.

The symptoms of perimenopause are different for every woman. Some women have an effortless time, while others experience severe symptoms. During our first discussion, my doctor warned me that given my history of thyroid issues, digestive struggles, and severe PMS throughout my life, I was going to have a difficult time. (Aren't I lucky?)

Because my doctor assured me that I wasn't *"sick,"* it was just the way my body reacted to hormonal changes, for the first year, I tried to tough it out without help. When I realized that I couldn't live my life without some assistance, I began taking natural supplements and vitamins and seeing my chiropractor more often. All of these things helped, but honestly, it's still been a difficult time for me.

Being completely honest, when this process began, I prayed that God would take it away and heal me. My life was in a really good season, and I didn't want these crazy symptoms interfering with my schedule or slowing me down. Much like the Apostle Paul, who begged God to take away his thorn in the flesh, I pleaded with God that the symptoms would disappear.

Instead of answering my prayer, God gave me this Scripture: *"But he said to me, 'My grace is sufficient for you, for my power is made perfect in weakness.' Therefore I will boast all the more gladly about my weaknesses, so that Christ's power may rest on me. That is why, for Christ's sake, I delight in weaknesses, in insults, in hardships, in persecutions, in difficulties. For when I am weak, then I am strong." (2 Corinthians 12:9-10, NIV)*

Okay, so it wasn't really what I wanted to hear. But it was exactly what I needed to hear.

You see, what God knew but I didn't, was that this challenge, like all trials, would help me learn and grow more than I could have ever imagined. It taught me so many things about myself and how I wanted to live my life. While the physical symptoms are challenging, I've learned so much about myself through the struggle. It's been a blessing. (If you remind me of that the next time I'm having a hot flash, I might slap you, but it's still true.)

The fact is that *"the change"* dramatically changed me. It put a spotlight on areas where I needed to change and set me free from thinking patterns that were holding me back from experiencing the abundant life Jesus had for me. So while the dear ladies in my perimenopause support group will still hear me complaining about the crazy symptoms, deep in my heart,

I know that God has allowed this time for my good.

However, I cannot deny that it's been hard. In the next few chapters, I'm going to share some of the specific lessons that I've learned through this time. However, before we go further, I wanted to share some of the lessons I've learned that have helped me deal with the physical symptoms that go along with PMS and perimenopause.

One of the lessons I've learned through my lifelong struggle with PMS and perimenopause is that the Heavenly Father cares very much for women and their physical struggles. We see this in the story of the woman with the issue of blood in Luke 8.

The Bible tells her that she had been bleeding for twelve years. I honestly cannot imagine how hard this was! Day and night, the disease in her body dominated her days and consumed her mind. She tried to function as well as she could, but ultimately, her sickness limited her. The constant loss of blood left her body weak and exhausted. Living with hormones that never balanced themselves affected her mind and emotions. Because Jewish culture deemed women who were menstruating "unclean," she had to live with that stigma. Her illness interfered with her marriage, her family, her friendships, and her ability to worship God at the Temple. When she came to Jesus, she was desperate for help.

The beautiful thing is the way that Jesus responded to her. First, he recognized her genuine need. Let's be honest ladies, this is a big deal, especially for anyone who has ever heard to *"Get over it, it's just PMS."* Instead, Jesus recognized that this woman was suffering, and her physical symptoms were real. He didn't mock her, make fun of her, or treat her problem as trivial. Instead, Jesus treated her with respect, and He had compassion on her. He made time for her, and He healed her.

It's so important that we recognize Jesus' circumstances when He stopped to talk to this woman. As we read the rest of the chapter, we see that Jesus and the crowd following Him were on their way to heal the dying daughter of a prominent ruler. I'm sure many in the group were annoyed that Jesus stopped to help the woman when they thought He should have focused on the life and death of this little girl. To them, nothing could be more critical, but to Jesus, this woman and her *"feminine problem"* were important.

Look at how He treated this woman. He spoke tenderly to her and called her *"Daughter."*

He showed her compassion, concern, and understanding.

He stopped everything just to help her.

As I've struggled through the years, first with extreme PMS, and now with perimenopause, I've learned that Jesus wants to be there for us in the same way. He wants to help each of us as we go through our feminine issues. To Him, women and what we go through is important. As we have our problems with PMS, pregnancy, postpartum depression, and perimenopause, He shows us the same compassion, concern, and understanding He showed her.

Secondly, I believe it's essential to understand that God

wants to help us through this time in life. Because He created our bodies, He understands them. No matter our symptoms or struggles, He wants to be there for us, showing the same love, care, and concern that He showed to the woman with the issue of blood. Even though He may not instantly take away our symptoms as He did with her, He is still there to help, to listen, and be with us through this time. Beyond a shadow of a doubt, I know I could not have made it through this time without Him.

So the next time you are struggling, try to take a moment and remember that Jesus wants to help you. Talk to Him, tell Him how you are feeling. Ask Him for His help to get through this time.

Remember, you are so important to Jesus. He loves you and wants to help you just like He did the woman in Luke 8. Reach out to Him for help like she did. He will be there for you.

Here are a few other practical tips I've learned for dealing with this interesting stage in life:

1. Be honest with yourself and the people around you about what you are going through.

How often have you been going through a hormonal day when someone close to you asked if you're feeling hormonal? (Such a dangerous question!) Of course, our natural response is, *"No! Can't I just have a bad day? Why do you have to blame everything on hormones?"*

Then you get angry when they reply, *"Well, you're crying*

over Cheerios that fell on the floor, and that isn't typically something you'd do, so is it possible that it might be hormones?"

Yep. Been there; done that. I learned a long time ago, that when I'm experiencing PMS or other hormonal symptoms, it's best to admit it and let the people around me know that I'm having a bad day. I've found that they are a lot more understanding when we acknowledge that we aren't feeling well than when we deny there is a problem.

2. You Don't Have to Go Through This Alone.

About a year into perimenopause, I met another woman who was in the same season of life. Soon, she gathered a bunch of her friends together to form a Facebook group where we could all support each other. While I've never personally met most of the women in the group, I am grateful for them all. On days when I feel like I'm all alone in this struggle, I can make a post and be reminded that I'm normal, that we're all going through the same things, and that we're all going to make it. Filled with some humor, some sarcasm, and a mutual disdain for this time in life, we support each other and help each other through this wild season.

3. Remember, this too shall pass.

My friend often says, *"Look at all the women who are older than us. They made it through and are enjoying their lives, and we'll make it, too."*

As I talk with older friends and remember my Mom's experience with menopause, I remember that this is only a season. Like all seasons, it will end. Someday we'll look back on it, and it will only be a memory. For me, that time can't come soon enough!

Write in your journal how these verses apply to this chapter's topic:

"A woman in the crowd had suffered for twelve years with constant bleeding, and she could find no cure. Coming up behind Jesus, she touched the fringe of his robe. Immediately, the bleeding stopped.

'Who touched me?' Jesus asked.

Everyone denied it, and Peter said, 'Master, this whole crowd is pressing up against you.'

But Jesus said, 'Someone deliberately touched me, for I felt healing power go out from me.'

When the woman realized that she could not stay hidden, she began to tremble and fell to her knees in front of him. The whole crowd heard her explain why she had touched him and that she had been immediately healed. 'Daughter,' he said to her, 'your faith has made you well. Go in peace.'" (Luke 8:43-48, NLT)

"As a father has compassion on his children, so the Lord has compassion on those who fear him for he knows how we are formed, he remembers that we are dust." (Psalm 103:13-14, NIV)

"Because of these surpassingly great revelations. Therefore, in order to keep me from becoming conceited, I was given a thorn in my flesh, a messenger of Satan, to torment me.

Three times I pleaded with the Lord to take it away from me.

But he said to me, 'My grace is sufficient for you, for my power is made perfect in weakness.' Therefore I will boast all the more gladly about my weaknesses, so that Christ's power may rest on me.

That is why, for Christ's sake, I delight in weaknesses, in insults, in hardships, in persecutions, in difficulties. For when I am weak, then I am strong." (2 Corinthians 12:7-10, NIV)

Chapter 16

Be Kind To Yourself

"You need to give yourself the same kindness and compassion you extend to others. You need it, too."

One of the roles that I have always played best in life is caretaker. During my late twenties and early thirties, when my Mom and brother were having extreme physical difficulties, my calling in life was to help them, to help take care of our house, and to make their life easier. Before long, I realized that I wasn't just good at it, but I enjoyed it. I liked making other people's lives better and dedicating my life to helping others. Although I can't say that it was always easy, serving others did fill me with a sense of joy.

Even after my Mom passed away, I continued finding joy in helping people. I'd volunteer for projects at church, try to find ways to make others feel special, and always be there when someone needed a listening ear. Caretaking was my niche—where I was comfortable and knew I could serve God and others.

Then came perimenopause and so many new things to learn about myself! One of the first things I had to learn was that I needed to start being as kind to myself as I was to others. As a perfectionist who derived her value from accomplishments and the approval of other people, this was hard for me!! And yet, learning this lesson has changed my life.

The first way that I needed to learn to be kind to myself was very practical. I had to change how I ate—choosing healthier foods. (I wasn't fanatical—this girl still likes her chocolate. I just tried to make wiser choices.)

I started drinking more water.

I found nutritional supplements that worked for me.

A weekly trip to the chiropractor became a lifeline.

One significant change was that I needed to permit myself to rest. For me, this wasn't as easy as it sounds because it meant more than just getting eight hours of sleep. Instead, it meant that I had to give myself permission to relax, permission to take a nap if necessary, to have a pajama day, to turn off social media, and to let my mind rest when needed. I had to learn to say *"no"* to unnecessary things and not overwhelm my schedule. Some days I just had to let myself off the hook and say, *"I did the best that I could....that has to be enough."* I could no longer push myself to the edge of exhaustion, trying to prove that I was good enough. I had to learn balance and realize that life is better when you take better care of yourself.

Of course, being physically kind to myself was only part of the change that I had to make. The most significant way that I had to learn to be kind to myself was that I needed to stop talking negatively to myself about myself. Trust me, before this season of life, I was my own worst critic. One of the truths this challenging time taught me is that I need to extend the same kindness to myself that I always gave to others.

For instance, there are so many things that I would never say to another person, especially if they were going through a hard time or struggling physically.

I'd never say:

"Why do you have to be so lazy? It doesn't matter how you feel—get up and do something."

"Why are you so fat and ugly?"

"Why are you so stupid?"

"Can't you see that everyone else is more accomplished than you? Compared to them, you have no value at all."

These are things that we would never say!!! And yet, too many of us say these things to ourselves day after day. It is wrong, and it needs to stop.

Instead, we need to extend ourselves the same kindness,

concern, and compassion that we give to other people. Obviously, I'm not talking about giving ourselves a free pass to sin or live irresponsibly. We never have an excuse to live against the principles of God's Word. Instead, I'm saying that there is no need to beat ourselves up if the dishes don't get done until morning, or we need to take a nap. When we have to decline a request to volunteer or can't meet everyone's expectations all the time, we need to extend ourselves the same grace we would give to someone else who said, *"I'm having a physical issue...can I have a rain check?"*

The Bible says:

> **"Be merciful, just as your Father is merciful."**
> **(Luke 6:36, NIV)**

Doesn't it make sense that every once in a while, we should be merciful towards ourselves? A big part of this is purposefully putting an end to the negative self-talk. Instead, begin speaking positively to yourself about yourself.

Congratulate yourself for the things you did accomplish.

Thank God for the changes He is making in your life.

Learn to respect yourself as a daughter of God, who is deeply loved by her Heavenly Father.

When you have a bad day, learn to forgive yourself, get up the next day, and try again.

Ask the Holy Spirit to teach you to care for yourself the way we know we should care for others.

Be Kind To Yourself

Be kind—give yourself the same kindness and compassion you extend to others. You need it, too.

Write in your journal how these verses apply to this chapter's topic:

"Be kind and compassionate to one another, forgiving each other, just as in Christ God forgave you" (Ephesians 4:32, NIV)

"But the fruit of the Spirit is love, joy, peace, forbearance, kindness, goodness, faithfulness," (Galatians 5:22, NIV)

"Be merciful, just as your Father is merciful." (Luke 6:36, NIV)

Chapter 17

You Can't Do Everything

"Being forty taught me, you can't do everything—prioritize the things that only you can do."

It was late August, the end of a particularly busy summer. I'd spent most of my days writing and assembling the *"Finding Healing"* Book. On the weekends, we were traveling to speak at churches. Of course, I still had all of the usual work that goes with maintaining a ministry and a home. As summer came to an end, I was feeling exhausted and battling other symptoms related to perimenopause.

Still, there was one thing that kept gnawing at me: we still hadn't canned tomatoes. We **always** canned tomatoes. When my mom was alive and had severe environmental allergies, we canned all kinds of fruits and vegetables in huge quantities. Even though I'd cut back on freezing and canning since then, I was so upset with myself that summer would soon be ending, and I still hadn't gotten around to canning tomatoes.

Finally, tired of thinking about it, I asked my Dad, who would be driving right past the farmer's market, to bring home four half bushels of tomatoes. (Because why just buy one basket when you can buy four?)

The day the tomatoes arrived, so did a monster headache. It was so bad I felt nauseous every time I stood up. Only now, my kitchen was filled with hundreds of tomatoes.

Feeling overwhelmed by the headache, the enormity of the job in front of me, and fluctuating hormones, I started to cry. This was no whimper. It was a big, ugly cry. I just didn't know what else to do.

Still crying, I called my friend and mentor to pray that I would feel better so I could jar what had now become, in my opinion, the *"stupid tomatoes"*. Along with her prayer, she included a lecture on priorities and a question, *"What would happen if you didn't jar the tomatoes?"*

She laughed when I said through my tears, *"We could just eat the forty jars I have leftover in the basement from last year and then go to the grocery store if we needed more."*

On the other hand, if I didn't obey the Holy Spirit and write *"Finding Healing,"* it wouldn't have been written.

If we didn't travel to preach on the weekends, we wouldn't be fulfilling our calling.

You Can't Do Everything

If we didn't do the administrative work, the ministry would shut down fast. All of these were things I had to do—tomatoes didn't fit those criteria.

It was incidents like this (yeah, there were others) that taught me that you couldn't do everything—you need to prioritize the things that only you can do.

Before forty (and in perimenopause), I said *"yes"* to everything. Mentally, I equated "no" with failure or weakness. When I started experiencing really difficult perimenopause symptoms, I had to prioritize the things that only I could do, the things I wanted to do, and the things that would go on without me. More importantly, I had to learn to forgive myself for not being able to do everything and find my value in more than overachieving at my *"to-do"* list.

This applied to more areas than just tomatoes. (That was just the funniest. Imagine me sitting in a room filled with tomatoes, crying because I was too sick to can them!) The less funny stories came when I was overbooking and double booking my speaking schedule to prove that I was a legitimate minister and then being seriously ill through all of the events.

Really, the problem was inside of me. I found my value and worth from being busy, having a full calendar, knocking things off of my *"to-do"* list, and doing everything I thought a woman was supposed to do. When perimenopause arrived, and I had to start prioritizing my calendar, the real issue was that I had to find my value outside of my ability *"to do"*.

I had to be vulnerable and trust that people would like me even if I wasn't volunteering for every job. (By the way, some did not, and I had to learn to find better friends.) I also had to trust that God would continue to open the doors that He wanted me to go through even if I wasn't always promoting myself by being everywhere.

I had to step back, take a breath, learn to prioritize, and still value myself even if I wasn't overachieving (or achieving much at all).

At first, it wasn't easy. There was an adrenaline rush in the chaos and a feeling of accomplishment in the crazy schedule.

However, as time went on, I found there was peace in the calmness of a manageable schedule. Not just the peace that comes from rest, but the peace that comes from knowing that God still loves me even if I'm not *"accomplishing."* I've found peace in having friends who love me for who I am, not just for how I can help or serve them.

I've learned that *"no"* is a beautiful word and that I am only required to do the things that God called me to do. Everything else is just my attempt to fill a need inside of me that can only be filled by God.

Looking back now, I can see that God has been trying to teach me this lesson for years. It took perimenopause to finally make me realize that my value is not tied to what I do. My value comes from being a child of God.

Whether or not you are struggling with a physical issue, this is an important lesson for all women As long as we base our sense of worth on how much we can do, what we look like, who loves us, or what other people say about us, we will

You Can't Do Everything

always be building on a shaky foundation. Much like the parable in Matthew 7:24-27 about a man who built his house on the sand, whenever we base our value or sense of self-worth on fleeting things, we are in danger of a crash. It's when we find our value and sense of worth in the stability of God's love that we are truly secure.

How do we do this?

We begin building on the firm foundation when we invest in our personal relationship with Jesus—-spending time with Him, pouring out our heart to Him, listening to Him as He speaks to us in times of prayer, and through His Word. When we read the Bible and absorb God's truth into our lives, it renews our minds and helps us find our acceptance, our security, and our value in our relationship with our Heavenly Father.

These are the things that help us firmly grasp hold of the truth that each of us is only required to do the things that God calls us to do in life—no more or no less. This helps you set reasonable boundaries knowing that you don't get extra credit for doing *"all of the things."* Your Heavenly Father only wants you to do what He has designed and called you to do. When it comes to these things, He will give you all the strength, health, and wisdom that you need to accomplish the task.

Matthew 11:28-30 says, ***"Come to me, all you who are weary and burdened, and I will give you rest. Take my yoke upon you and learn from me, for I am gentle and humble in heart, and you will find rest for your souls. For my yoke*** *is easy and my burden is light."*

The truth is that God never meant for us to do everything to earn His love. He doesn't want us to be overburdened and exhausted, carrying burdens that He didn't design for us. Instead, He wants us to come to Him, spend time with Him, allow Him to direct our lives, and then only do the things that He has called us to do.

At one point in life, God called me to take care of my family and can tomatoes. He didn't ask me to write and speak and travel then. Now that He is calling me to do these things, I can't still do all of the things that I did before. And that's ok. Because I'm only responsible for doing what God is calling me to do right now. (If I have extra time maybe I'll can tomatoes in moderation—-that's another word perimenopause taught me).

The point is that when we find rest in Jesus, we realize that our value isn't about what we do. Our value comes from Him. This truth enables us to take a deep breath, relax, seek His will, and only carry the burdens that He designs for us. When we do this, we avoid the overwhelming, exhausting rat race of trying to "earn" our value. We simply know that we are valuable because we belong to Jesus. This sets us free to ask, *"What does God want me to do?"*, then do it.

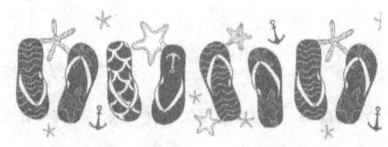

Write in your journal how these verses apply to this chapter's topic:

"Come to me, all you who are weary and burdened, and I will give you rest. Take my yoke upon you and learn from me, for I am gentle and humble in heart, and you will find rest for your souls. For my yoke is easy and my burden is light." (Matthew 11:28-30, NIV)

"Therefore everyone who hears these words of mine and puts them into practice is like a wise man who built his house on the rock. The rain came down, the streams rose, and the winds blew and beat against that house; yet it did not fall, because it had its foundation on the rock. But everyone who hears these words of mine and does not put them into practice is like a foolish man who built his house on sand. The rain came down, the streams rose, and the winds blew and beat against that house, and it fell with a great crash." (Matthew 5:24-27, NIV)

"For it is by grace you have been saved, through faith—and this is not from yourselves, it is the gift of God—not by works, so that no one can boast. For we are God's handiwork, created in Christ Jesus to do good works, which God prepared in advance for us to do." (Ephesians 2:8-10, NIV)

"Are not two sparrows sold for a penny? Yet not one of them will fall to the ground outside your Father's care. And even the *very hairs of your head are all numbered. So don't be afraid; you are worth more than many sparrows." (Matthew 10:29-31, NIV)*

Chapter 18

Life's Not A Competition

"Being 40 taught me that comparison is a HUGE waste of time and energy. The world is big enough for us all to succeed."

Before perimenopause, I was very competitive. When I saw someone else succeed, I compared myself to her and viewed myself as a failure. When hot flashes and dizzy spells made me realize that there was a limit on what I could do, I began to see how ridiculous it is to live life this way. Before perimenopause, it was a different story.

Looking back on my life, I guess I've always been a competitive person. Even as a child, I wanted to be the best at everything. It wasn't enough to be in the school play; I wanted the lead. I didn't just sing in the choir—I soloed. Academically, I took great pride in the fact that I was working several years above my grade level. In almost every area of my

Ageless Truths

life (except sports—I was terrible at sports) I wanted to be the first, the best, the winner. Everything was a competition.

As I grew older, the pattern of seeing other women as competition continued to grow. It was like I was keeping a chart in my head. I was intimidated whenever I came across a woman who was more successful in any area of life. If I was doing better than another woman, I felt superior. Comparison was the scorecard that I used to determine my value in life.

Unfortunately, I carried this terrible trait with me in my early ministry life. Rather than seeing other women in ministry as comrades, too often, I saw them as competitors. The winner was the one who got the most compliments after they taught a class, sold the most books, or got the most prominent speaking engagement. If your calendar was full when mine was empty, I felt intimidated. If my schedule was full, I had a brief moment of peace before I started worrying about keeping it filled for the next year.

As I said in the last chapter, I got my value and self-worth from all the wrong places. After years of following God down a path that made me feel like a failure, I felt like I had a lot to prove. Like a runner coming from behind, I was trying extra hard to prove that I belonged in the race.

Let me tell you —-it was exhausting!! Between the self-flagellation when I wasn't as good as another person (which happened quite frequently) and the constant effort I put into being more successful than other women, I wasted way too much emotional energy.

Life's Not A Competition

Thankfully, God used the trying season of perimenopause to help me overcome this terrible trait once and for all.

How did it happen? As we talked about in the last chapter, the physical symptoms of perimenopause made me realize that I couldn't do everything. I couldn't be everywhere. After too many attempts at overbooking my calendar only to end up feeling ill, I realized something had to change.

These changes took me out of the competition. Physically, I couldn't keep up. I could only do what God allowed me to do—not what I wanted to do to prove that I was good enough.

Even though I hated this at first, God knew it was the absolute best thing for me. As I said in the last chapter, it forced me to stop the competition and find my value and self-worth in Jesus. It taught me that I am worthy; I am loved; I am good enough simply because God loves me. It didn't matter how much I could do or how I stacked up to someone else. I have value simply because I am His daughter. As long as I follow Jesus and walk in His plan for my life, it doesn't matter how I compare to others.

I love the conversation between Jesus and Peter in John 21:20-23, where Peter sees John and asks Jesus, *"What about him?"* Very much like He responded to Peter, the Holy Spirit eventually taught me that it doesn't matter what God calls other people to do—I need to follow Jesus. I am called to run my race, stay in my lane, and let others do the same.

Carolyn Tenant's book *"Catch the Wind of the Spirit"* [1] compares the kingdom of God to a choreographed dance where all of the dancers take turns moving in and out of the spotlight. The beauty of the dance is found in every dancer performing their part in coordination with the others.

This visual made an impression on my mind reminding me that this is how the kingdom of God works. We are all meant to serve God, flowing in our unique calling according to God's timing. Walking the steps assigned to us, God coordinates all of our movements in a way that advances His kingdom and brings as many people as possible into a personal relationship with Jesus.

We aren't called to compete with one another or be jealous of another person's role. Instead, we are called to play our part by walking in our unique calling and cheering on others as they walk in their unique calling.

Because it isn't about me, and it isn't about you. We are all called to reflect Jesus, to advance God's kingdom, and to help people come to know Him.

Some days this means walking through the big door and shining in the spotlight. Other times we are in a supporting role, and other days we are backstage in our sweats, with no makeup, and our hair in a ponytail cheering for the rest of the team.

Over the past few years, one of the opportunities God provided that helped drive this truth home to me was when He allowed me to help other women promote and grow their ministries. As I've helped other women publish their books, build their websites, or develop their ministries, I've found the joy of working as a team. I've loved being able to work

Life's Not A Competition

behind the scenes to help their dreams become a reality. Whenever I hear a testimony of how their book or their class touched someone, I find so much fulfillment in knowing that I got to play a little part. Along the way, I've made some wonderful friends with people I might have previously seen as competitors. Now that I realize we are on the same team, I love standing on the sidelines and cheering, *"Way to go, girl!"*

It's paramount that we remember: our goal is to see our team win. To effectively fulfill the Great Commission, we need all hands on deck. The more people walking in their unique God-given calling, the more people are being reached, and the more hearts are changed.

In light of the Great Commission, we realize that life isn't a competition. There is more than enough work for all of us to do. When one person succeeds, we all succeed.

From a personal perspective, life is better when you choose to be a cheerleader instead of a competitor. When you realize that God's kingdom is a team, you have the freedom to play your role and allow others to play theirs. As we work together, God's will is accomplished.

In light of eternity, that's really all that matters.

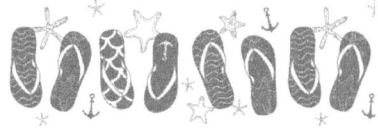

Write in your journal how these verses apply to this chapter's topic:

"Turning his head, Peter noticed the disciple Jesus loved following right behind. When Peter noticed him, he asked Jesus, 'Master, what's going to happen to him?'

Jesus said, 'If I want him to live until I come again, what's that to you? You—follow me.' That is how the rumor got out among the brothers that this disciple wouldn't die. But that is not what Jesus said. He simply said, 'If I want him to live until I come again, what's that to you?'" (John 21:20-23, MSG)

"Just as a body, though one, has many parts, but all its many parts form one body, so it is with Christ. For we were all baptized by one Spirit so as to form one body—whether Jews or Gentiles, slave or free—and we were all given the one Spirit to drink. Even so the body is not made up of one part but of many.

Now if the foot should say, 'Because I am not a hand, I do not belong to the body,' it would not for that reason stop being part of the body. And if the ear should say, 'Because I am not an eye, I do not belong to the body,' it would not for that reason stop being part of the body. If the whole body were an eye, where would the sense of hearing be? If the whole body were an ear, where would the sense of smell be? But in fact God has placed the parts in the body, every one of them, just as he wanted them to be. If they were all one part, where would the body be? As it is, there are many parts, but one body.

The eye cannot say to the hand, 'I don't need you!' And the head cannot say to the feet, 'I don't need you!'

On the contrary, those parts of the body that seem to be weaker are indispensable, and the parts that we think are less honorable we treat with special honor. And the parts that are unpresentable are treated with special modesty, while our presentable parts need no special treatment. But God has put the body together, giving greater honor to the parts that lacked it, so that there should be no division in the body, but that its parts should have equal concern for each other.

If one part suffers, every part suffers with it; if one part is honored, every part rejoices with it.

Now you are the body of Christ, and each one of you is a part of it". (1 Corinthians 12:12-27, NIV)

"*Then the eleven disciples went to Galilee, to the mountain where Jesus had told them to go. When they saw him, they worshiped him; but some doubted. Then Jesus came to them and said, 'All authority in heaven and on earth has been given to me. Therefore go and make disciples of all nations, baptizing them in the name of the Father and of the Son and of the Holy Spirit, and teaching them to obey everything I have commanded you. And surely I am with you always, to the very end of the age.'" (Matthew 28:16-20, NIV)*

"*For by the grace given me I say to every one of you: Do not think of yourself more highly than you ought, but rather think of yourself with sober judgment, in accordance with the faith God has distributed to each of you.*

For just as each of us has one body with many members, and these members do not all have the same function, so in Christ we, though many, form one body, and each member belongs to all the others. We have different gifts, according to the grace given to each of us. If your gift is prophesying, then prophesy in accordance with your faith; if it is serving, then serve; if it is teaching, then teach; if it is to encourage, then give encouragement; if it is giving, then give generously; if it is to lead, do it diligently; if it is to show mercy, do it cheerfully.

Love must be sincere. Hate what is evil; cling to what is good. Be devoted to one another in love. Honor one another above yourselves." (Romans 12:3-10, NIV)

Chapter 19

You Really Need to Learn to Laugh

"For what do we live, but to make sport for our neighbors, and laugh at them in our turn?" -Jane Austin, Pride & Prejudice [1]

I love this quote from Jane Austin's *"Pride and Prejudice."* I have to admit that I've quoted it far too often since I first watched the BBC's miniseries many years ago. It sums up the feeling, *"Why not let people laugh at the silly things we do? We're funny...why not enjoy it?"*

This is an attitude that was once again a result of the wonderful process of perimenopause, although I wasn't the one going through this dreadful time. Instead, this truth became part of our family dynamic when my Mom went through perimenopause in her late thirties.

I'm not going to lie. This was a difficult time for our family. Being only thirty-six when she started experiencing dramatic symptoms, the doctors assured her that she could not be starting menopause. They put her through many medical tests for many years before she finally found a doctor who confirmed that everything she was suffering was the result of her change in life. Yet, through this time, it wasn't just my Mom's hormones that were changing. God was using this time to change her, too.

One of the most significant changes was that my Mom was learning to laugh. Until this point, Mom was a pretty serious person. She had a tough childhood and was in a problematic marriage filled with stress. It was imperative to both her and my Dad that things always *"looked good."* For all of her excellent qualities, before menopause, she took herself and life too seriously.

Then came *"the change,"* and things were beyond her control. That's when Mom learned to laugh—-at herself, at life, at what was happening around her. As the saying goes, *"When Mama's happy, the family is happy."* (Okay, that's not exactly how it goes, but you get the idea.)

When my Mom learned to stop taking life so seriously, to laugh and enjoy the ride, it changed the entire dynamic of our family. We all learned to laugh. This is how God answered my Mom's prayer when she first became a Christian that *"laughter would fill the walls of our home."*

Looking back now, some of my fondest memories of spending time with my Mom were when we were laughing together. In fact, laughter became such a stable in her personality that after she went to Heaven, a friend of our family said, *"I just loved your Mom's laugh—she had a great laugh."*

The ability to laugh at life, at yourself, and circumstances, helped my family and me through some of the hardest times in our lives. There's something about laughter that finds a break in the tension and releases some of the pressure. Laughter helps you take a deep breath, regain your courage, and find the strength to go on even in the most difficult of circumstances.

Again, this was something I learned from my Mom: she used laughter to deal with stress. I remember one Saturday afternoon when I was about twelve years old, Mom and Dad decided we would take a drive to look at the changing autumn leaves in upstate Pennsylvania. It was a beautiful day, until the car's engine completely died on an interstate in the middle of nowhere. Of course, my Dad reacted the way he usually did and ran into the woods to be sick. My Mom waited by the broken car with two kids laughing her head off!

That's when a truck driver stopped to see if he could call someone to help the poor woman and children with the broken car. Ironically, that's when my Dad came storming down out of the trees.

You should have seen the terrified look on that truck driver's face! He thought he was being ambushed! Quickly, my Mom explained that it was only her husband—he was sick. Of course, the ridiculousness of that situation made her laugh even more.

Over the years, Jamie and I came to appreciate my Mom's ability to cope with stress this way. I can't tell you how often laughter has helped alleviate stressful situations and put things into perspective.

Carrying on the tradition, I've learned to use laughter as a coping mechanism when facing difficult times. (Remember the story of being stuck in the sand at the beach?) Although I try not to be inappropriate (although sometimes I laugh at inopportune times), part of my process in dealing with stress is finding something in the situation that causes laughter. It's not that I'm ignoring the seriousness of the issue, I've just learned that laughter helps clear your head so you can deal with serious problems.

Another way that learning to laugh has helped me is in learning not to take myself so seriously. The truth is that when I was younger, I took myself WAY too seriously. It was very important to me that I always appeared to have it all together. When I made a mistake, failed at something, didn't live up to my expectations, or God forbid, did something embarrassing, it was the end of the world! Catastrophic! Looking back now, I think, "What a waste of time and energy!" But back then, the need to appear *"perfect"* was genuine.

It wasn't until I came home from college that I was finally able to learn this lesson from my Mom: You need to learn to laugh at yourself.

The truth is that you're not perfect (not even close), but

You Really Need to Learn to Laugh

your imperfections are funny.

Everyone does silly things. Everyone fails.

Everyone spills things. Everyone trips over things they should have seen.

We all say inappropriate things, do ridiculous things, make mistakes that shouldn't be made, and all of our bodies make sounds they shouldn't make in public.

Life happens. When it does, we can either be uptight and embarrassed, or we can learn to laugh at ourselves.

This is something I learned to do by watching my Mom. I listened as she would tell a joke that wasn't really that funny, and then laugh at it so hard that you'd start laughing, too. I laughed as she put things into perspective with her sense of humor. I saw her laugh at herself and her mistakes, and this taught me to do the same.

Honestly, that's what really changed me: I consciously chose to change my attitude and start laughing at myself. Even more, I started allowing and even inviting others to laugh with me.

In fact, one of the first things I started writing and sharing online was called *"The Crazy Lady's Corner."* In these blogs, I'd share the absolutely ridiculous things that happened to me and all of the stupid things that I did. Later, when social media became a part of our lives, I determined that I wouldn't just share what made me look good, but I would also share the silly, the stupid, the clumsy, and the downright comical parts of my life. Much like the Pride and Prejudice quote, I figured if I enjoyed a laugh from an incident, than my friends probably would as well.

As I learned to laugh at myself and share that laughter with others, some interesting things happened. First, it helped me learn to be myself, to accept myself, to relax in who God made me, and to enjoy my life much more. Anyone who struggles with the pressure always to appear *"perfect,"* to hide behind masks, and to look like you have it all together, will testify that this is a lot of pressure. Learning to laugh at myself and allowing other people to laugh at me set me free from so much of this nonsense. It was life-changing.

It's actually been medicinal as it has relieved so much stress and tension from my life and replaced it with joy. It's made me a happier, healthier, more emotionally, and mentally balanced person. As Proverbs 17:22 says, ***"A cheerful heart is good medicine, but a crushed spirit dries up the bones." (NIV)***

The other thing that I learned was that when I let my hair down and made self-deprecating humor a part of my life, rather than rejecting me because I didn't have it all together, people liked me more. When I was vulnerable, they felt that they were free to be vulnerable. As I relaxed, so did other people. When I let my guard down, other people let there's down, too. This actually led to stronger, healthier relationships with friends and family. It also opened more doors for me to be able to reach people with the message of hope that is found in Jesus.

You Really Need to Learn to Laugh

The truth is that few people can relate to perfect people. It's difficult to be in a relationship with someone who never lets you see their vulnerable side and avoids showing their humanity. On the other hand, laughter breaks down many of those walls and opens so many doors as people see that you are just like them: human. And humans are funny.

That's why whenever someone asks me advice on how to live your best life, one of the things I say is: You really need to learn to laugh.

Realize you are funny. Actually, you're hysterical.

Learn to laugh at yourself and let others laugh with you.

Life is a lot more fun that way. (For you and everyone around you.) Trust me.

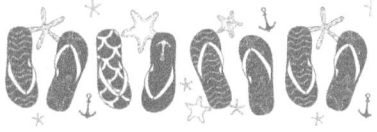

Write in your journal how these verses apply to this chapter's topic:

"She is clothed with strength and dignity; she can laugh at the days to come." (Proverbs 31:25, NIV)

"A cheerful heart is good medicine, but a crushed spirit dries up the bones." (Proverbs 17:22, NIV)

(There's) "a time to weep and a time to laugh," (Ecclesiastes 3:4, NIV)

"Our mouths were filled with laughter, our tongues with songs of joy. Then it was said among the nations, 'The Lord has done great things for them.'" (Psalms 126:2, NIV)

Chapter 20

You're Never Too Old To Be Daddy's Girl

"No matter what your experience with your earthly father, the Heavenly Father wants to teach you how to be a daughter."

I stepped off the stage after speaking to a group of women when I saw the text. Thinking it would be a word of encouragement, I opened it. It was the exact opposite. Instead, someone I put a lot of faith in proved they weren't worthy of my trust. We made an agreement, signed contracts, and they decided not to honor their commitments. They assured me if I tried to hold them to their commitment, they would make my life miserable.

Immediately, the consequences of what I'd just read settled in my spirit. This was awful. As my mind raced toward the worst-case scenarios thinking about the fallout, I felt more than shaken, I was stunned.

How could someone I trusted do this? What would the future hold? What would the consequences be if they followed through on their threatening language?

It was around this time, as I went back and forth between shock and frenzied panic, that I came across a fellow minister. I remember she said that I looked like someone who had just been through a car accident. I guess it was similar because, in my heart, it felt like something had crashed.

That's when my friend began to pray a powerful prayer. As she prayed, she repeated these words, *"You are a child of God....God is Your Father....and He will take care of this."* As she prayed, I just cried and wondered if what she said was really true. The truth is that, at that moment, I didn't see how it was possible.

Over the next few weeks, the situation progressed slowly. At one point, I remember being alone in my room in prayer, laying the entire situation before God and saying:

"I honestly do not know what to do. I don't know how to fix this, and I don't see how You can fix it.

But what I do know is that I want to trust You. I know that You are perfect. I know that You love me. I know that even if the worst happens, You are trustworthy and You will bring something useful from this situation.

So I leave this whole situation in Your hands and trust that

You're Never Too Old To Be Daddy's Girl

You are My Father, and You will do what is best."

I truly laid everything at the altar, believing and hoping that what my friend said would be right and the Heavenly Father was trustworthy.

I wish I could say that I got up from that prayer, and everything was better. Instead, six weeks passed and then the phone rang. In a way that only God could arrange, the issue was resolved. Someone who had no idea the problem existed made a seemingly unrelated decision that eliminated the problem. Suddenly, I was protected and placed in a position where no weapon formed against me would prosper, and no wagging tongue could stand. (Isaiah 54:17)

Besides feeling shocked and awed, the most overwhelming thing that I felt was loved. Protected. Provided for.

I felt so safe in the arms of my Heavenly Father Who came to my rescue, provided my need, and delivered me from an enemy who wanted to cause destruction.

For me, this was a huge turning point. You see, throughout my life, I've had a complicated relationship with my Dad. I learned early in life that he wasn't going to take my side and stand up to other people. He was too concerned about what others would think. Even though I always knew I could count on my Mom (she was a real mama bear if anyone messed with one of her cubs), I always struggled to trust that I could rely on my Dad.

To a certain degree, this lack of trust carried over into my relationship with the Heavenly Father. Even though I knew

He could do all things, I always wondered if He would. Being completely honest, on the night that everything came crashing down and my friend said, *"God is your Father, He will handle this for you,"* there was a part of me that thought, *"We'll see."*

That's why this experience was so life-changing for me—because in a very tangible, personal way, God came through.

He moved mountains for me.

He turned people's hearts in my situation. In a desperate situation where I didn't know how to help myself, the Heavenly Father came in and rescued me. It wasn't something I read about in the Bible—I saw the miracle happen. And it changed me.

Through this period, I learned that you are never too old to be the Heavenly Father's daughter. No matter what your experience with your earthly father, the Heavenly Father wants to teach you how to be a daughter. He wants to protect you, provide for you, be your Defender and your Strength.

He is your Father in the corner, cheering for you, pulling for you to succeed. When you fall, He is there to pick you up, bandage your wounds, and help you heal.

He never leaves, and He never forsakes you. (Deuteronomy 31:6) He is reliable, dependable, and always, always trustworthy.

He wants what is best for us and works all things together for the good of His daughters so that we can fulfill our purpose in His kingdom.

We are never too old or too young to experience new facets of His love for us—to truly understand what it feels like to run into the Father's arms and feel His embrace.

Today, I don't know what you are going through. Perhaps your skies are sunny. Maybe you're going through the darkest storm of your life. Either way, can I encourage you to spend some time in the arms of your Heavenly Father today? Talk to Him, share your heart with Him, tell Him about all of your burdens, and ask Him to carry them for you. Spend some time reading the Bible and hearing Him speak to you.

Whatever you are going through, know beyond a shadow of a doubt that *"You are a child of God....God is Your Father....and He will take care of this."*

Remember, it's never too late to be a Daddy's girl because of the faithfulness of the Heavenly Father.

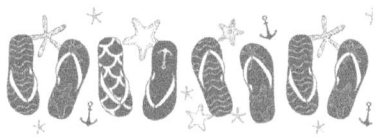

Ageless Truths

Write in your journal how these verses apply to this chapter's topic:

"God is our refuge and strength, an ever-present help in trouble. Therefore we will not fear, though the earth give way and the mountains fall into the heart of the sea, though its waters roar and foam and the mountains quake with their surging." *(Psalm 46:1-3, NIV)*

"One thing I ask from the Lord, this only do I seek: that I may dwell in the house of the Lord all the days of my life, to gaze on the beauty of the Lord. and to seek him in his temple.

For in the day of trouble he will keep me safe in his dwelling; he will hide me in the shelter of his sacred tent and set me high upon a rock." *(Psalm 27:1-5, NIV)*

"As a father has compassion on his children, so the Lord has compassion on those who fear him." *(Psalm 103:13, NIV)*

"Look at the birds of the air; they do not sow or reap or store away in barns, and yet your heavenly Father feeds them. Are you not much more valuable than they?" *(Matthew 6:26, NIV)*

Chapter 21

What Doesn't Kill You

"When we are constantly faced with the same issues over and over again, we need to realize that our only exit strategy is for us to once and for all overcome."

Hello. My name is Adessa, and I am a wimp.

A chicken. A coward.

When it comes to confrontation, I absolutely hate it!

I avoid it at all costs. The truth is that I often give people what they want rather than stand up for myself or say how I really feel. The thought of having to tell someone something they don't want to hear makes me physically sick. When it looks like there's going to be an argument, I'm more than likely to run away than actually face it.

This is me. I could go through the whole story, telling

you why I am this way and which of my relatives passed this trait onto me, but the truth is that, at this point, the details don't matter. I know what happened and why I am the way I am.

Here's another thing I know: The Heavenly Father does not like this part of my personality. I'd go so far as to say that He hates it.

Sound too drastic to you?

Well, I've got pretty convincing proof that God hates this defect in my personality: He is always trying to kill it and help me overcome it.

How is He trying to kill it?

Over and over throughout my forties, He keeps allowing situations in my life that require bravery, honesty, and, dare I say it, confrontation. Even though I've tried running away, avoiding confrontation, binding the enemy, praying about situations, and anything else I can find to *"fix"* different circumstances in my life, NOTHING WORKS!

God keeps allowing me to go through things where the only answer is to have an awkward conversation, be brave, take a risk, and stop being a wimp. I think He's going with the *"what doesn't kill you makes you stronger"* theory.

Especially as I entered my early forties, I was sure God had one mission: Make me stronger.

Of course, my initial reaction is to ask, *"Why do I have to keep going through the same trial? Different names, faces, and details, but always the same thing?"* It's the old *"Why can't God just love me the way I am?"* question.

Of course, the answer is that God does love me---He loves me too much to let me stay the way that I am. He knows that this particular quality is a defect in my personality. It's hurting me, and it's not healthy. Just like no doctor would let a patient with an injury stay injured, God cannot watch one of His children continue being unhealthy when He knows that some physical therapy will cause healing. Like a competent physician, he wants to see us healthier and better able to be the person He wants them to be and do what He has called them to do.

So He challenges us and makes us uncomfortable. He allows circumstances in our lives that attack the unhealthy, harmful things in our lives to demolish them and replace them with the fruit of the spirit in our lives.

This is true in my life. The enemy wants to use this area of weakness to destroy me, but my Heavenly Father knows that with the help of the Holy Spirit living inside of me, I will not be destroyed. Instead, these trials and struggles in my life will make me stronger---healthier---holier. That is the Heavenly Father's goal.

Hence, I am expecting more struggles, more confrontations, more times when I'm going to have to… GULP…speak the truth in love when it would be easier to run.

Why?

Because I know that God wants what is best for me, and being a wimp is not what is best.

So He'll keep putting me through spiritual therapy, making me stronger and wiser until the day I can say with certainty, *"My name is Adessa, and I am not afraid."*

What about you?

What struggles do you see reappearing in your life over and over again?

What makes you say, *"I can't believe I'm facing this again? Why does this keep happening to me?"*

Is it possible that God is allowing this struggle in your life because He sees things that He wants you to overcome?

Do you have weak areas where God is trying to make you stronger?

The truth is that nothing can touch a believer that does not first pass through God's hand. When we face the same issues over and over again, we need to realize that our only exit strategy is for us to once and for all overcome.

Look that challenge in the eye, see what God is doing inside of you, agree with Him that you do need to improve in that area and say, *"Bring it on!"* Let's kick this weakness to the curb and finally become the women that God wants us to be.

Are you with me? (Wow, that actually sounded, dare I say it, BRAVE!)

Write in your journal how these verses apply to this chapter's topic.

"The Sovereign Lord is my strength; he makes my feet like the feet of a deer, he enables me to tread on the heights." (Habakkuk 3:19, NIV)

"It is God who arms me with strength and keeps my way secure. He makes my feet like the feet of a deer; he causes me to stand on the heights.

He trains my hands for battle; my arms can bend a bow of bronze. You make your saving help my shield, and your right hand sustains me; your help has made me great.

You provide a broad path for my feet, so that my ankles do not give way." (Psalm 18:32-36, NIV)

"Praise be to the Lord my Rock, who trains my hands for war, my fingers for battle." (Psalm 144:1, NIV)

"You, dear children, are from God and have overcome them, because the one who is in you is greater than the one who is in the world." (1 John 4:4, NIV)

"No, despite all these things, overwhelming victory is ours through Christ, who loved us." (Romans 8:37, NLT)

Conclusion

And so our time together is coming to a close. I hope you've enjoyed our journey together. I hope you've laughed at some of my stories, that you've been able to relate to some of my feelings, and that you will choose to apply these ageless truths to your own life. I pray this book has inspired you to:

Be yourself.

Laugh frequently.

Love Jesus with total abandon.

Love God's Word and seek to obey it.

Most importantly, I hope this book helped you throw off the shackles of fear, lies, and insecurities that bind too many of us. To follow the words of Hebrews 12:1 and *"throw off everything that hinders and the sin that so easily entangles. And let us run with perseverance the race marked out for us". (NIV)*

Within these chapters, I pray that you've seen that you are not alone. You are surrounded by a sisterhood of Christian women facing the same battles, struggling with similar issues, and depending on the same Heavenly Father to help us find victory. Even though our demographics and our stories may be different, the ageless truths found in the Bible apply to us all. Whatever your age, these are the principles that will bring us healing from our past, freedom in our present, and hope and excitement as we walk into the future that God has for us.

Remember: you're never too young or too old to allow the Bible's ageless truths to revolutionize your life. Today and tomorrow, God's Word is there to be your Light, your Guide, and your Encouragement as you continue your journey toward becoming the woman God is calling you to be.

Thank you so much for sharing part of your journey with me. It's been a complete joy to share my journey with you.

Until Next Time,

Adessa

"Being confident of this, that he who began a good work in you will carry it on to completion until the day of Christ Jesus." (Philippians 1:6, NIV)

We're all just a little bit broken.

We all have areas from our past, from choices we've made, or from circumstances that we've lived through that have caused us pain and heartache in our lives.

The good news is that we don't have to stay trapped in our brokenness. Through the power of the Holy Spirit and practicing the Biblical principles of healing, each of us can experience victory, freedom, and the abundant life that Jesus has for us.

Visit **www.adessaholden.com** for details.

Also available in both print and digital formats from Amazon, BarnesandNoble.com, and other online retailers.

"Life is an adventure, you need to learn to love the journey."

But what if your journey doesn't resemble the life of your dreams? Can you still love the adventure God designs for you?

In this book, you'll find the answer is "Absolutely, Yes!"

Sharing practical principles learned on her own journey, Adessa supplies key advice and Biblical teaching that will help you discover your God-given passion, place and purpose and appreciate every step of the journey along the way….Are You Ready For The Adventure?

Visit **www.adessaholden.com** for details.

Also available in both print and digital formats from Amazon, BarnesandNoble.com, and other online retailers.

God has a plan for your life that is above and beyond anything you can imagine. He has a destiny He wants you to fulfill. A life that is so much richer and more meaningful than you could even dream. Now the choices lies with you.

Do you want to walk in God's call for your life? Do you want to find God's perfect will for your life, your destiny, the reason you were created and the job God has for you? As you discover your calling, are you willing to do whatever it takes to walk in your calling? If you are ready to say, "Yes!" this is the book for you. Visit **www.adessaholden.com** for details.

Also available in both print and digital formats from Amazon, BarnesandNoble.com, and other online retailers.

We all crave significance. Adessa Holden's book

FINDING SIGNIFICANCE

will help you understand how God sees you, that he loves to speak hope and new life into those that the world sees as insignificant. Each chapter provides questions for reflection, making it a wonderful tool for self or small group study.

Visit www.adessaholden.com for details.

Also available in both print and digital formats from Amazon, BarnesandNoble.com, and other online retailers.

About The Author

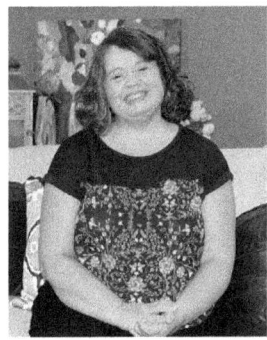

Adessa Holden is an author and an ordained minister with the Assemblies of God specializing in Women's Ministry. Together with her brother, Jamie, they manage 4One Ministries and travel the East Coast speaking, holding conferences and producing Men's and Women's resources that provide practical Biblical teaching for everyday life.

Adessa's passion is helping women develop an intimate, personal relationship with Jesus and become the women God originally designed them to be.

When asked about herself, she'll tell you, "I'm a women's minister, a sister, and a daughter. I love to laugh and spend time with people. My favorite things are chocolate, the ocean, sandals and white capris, anything purple, summertime, and riding in the car listening to music. (Which is a good thing considering how much time I spend traveling.)

It is my absolute honor and privilege to serve Jesus and women through this ministry."

Adessa can be contacted at: adessa@adessaholden.com.

Visit her website at: www.adessaholden.com.

Bibliography

Chapter 7

1. Tennant, Carolyn. Catch the Wind of the Spirit: How the 5 Ministry Gifts Can Transform Your Church. Springfield, MO: Vital Resources, 2016. Pg 87-100.

Chapter 12

1. Austen, Jane, Simon Langton, Sue Birtwistle, Colin Firth, and Jennifer Ehle. Pride and Prejudice. London: BBC Production, 1995.

Chapter 15

1. Russo, Anthony, Joe Russo, Christopher Markus, Stephen McFeely, Kevin Feige, Chris Evans, Robert Downey, Scarlett Johansson, Sebastian Stan, Anthony Mackie, Don Cheadle, Jeremy Renner, Chadwick Boseman, Paul Bettany, Elizabeth Olsen, Paul Rudd, Emily VanCamp, Marisa Tomei, Tom Holland, Frank Grillo, Martin Freeman, William Hurt, Daniel Brühl, Trent Opaloch, Jeffrey Ford, Matthew Schmidt, Henry Jackman, Joe Simon, and Jack Kirby. Captain America: Civil War. , 2016.

Chapter 18

1. Montgomery, L M. Anne of Green Gables. New York: Bantam Books, 1976. Pg 154.